Sweeter Than Honey,
Richer Than Gold

Reading the Bible as Literature

How Bible Stories Work: A Guided Study of Biblical Narrative

Sweeter Than Honey, Richer Than Gold: A Guided Study of Biblical Poetry

Letters of Grace & Beauty: A Guided Literary Study of New Testament Epistles

Jesus the Hero: A Guided Literary Study of the Gospels

Symbols & Reality: A Guided Study of Prophecy, Apocalypse, and Visionary Literature

Short Sentences Long Remembered: A Guided Study of Proverbs and Other Wisdom Literature

READING
THE BIBLE AS
LITERATURE

Sweeter Than Honey, Richer Than Gold

A GUIDED STUDY
OF BIBLICAL POETRY

LELAND RYKEN

LEXHAM PRESS

Sweeter Than Honey, Richer Than Gold: A Guided Study of Biblical Poetry
© 2015 by Leland Ryken

Lexham Press, 1313 Commercial St., Bellingham, WA 98225
LexhamPress.com

First edition by Weaver Book Company.

Print ISBN 9781683591542
Digital ISBN 9781683591559

Cover design and interior layout: Frank Gutbrod

Contents

Series Preface   7

Introduction:
What Is Biblical Poetry? And Why It Is Good for You   11

Part 1: The Language Poets Use

1. **First Things First:**
   The Primacy of the Image   21
2. **How Is A Like B?**
   The Use of Metaphor and Simile   35
3. **Make-Believe:**
   Poetry and the Nonliteral   49
4. **Artistic Beauty:**
   The Parallelism of Biblical Poetry   69

Part 2: The Composition of Biblical Poems

5. **What We Need to Know about Biblical Poems**   81
6. **Putting All the Pieces Together:**
   How to Explicate a Biblical Poem   103
7. **What Are the Main Types of Psalms?**   117

Series Preface

This series is part of the mission of the publisher to equip Christians to understand and teach the Bible effectively by giving them reliable tools for handling the biblical text. Within that landscape, the niche that my volumes are designed to fill is the literary approach to the Bible. This has been my scholarly passion for nearly half a century. It is my belief that a literary approach to the Bible is the common reader's friend, in contrast to more specialized types of scholarship on the Bible.

Nonetheless, the literary approach to the Bible needs to be defended against legitimate fears by evangelical Christians, and through the years I have not scorned to clear the territory of misconceptions as part of my defense of a literary analysis of the Bible. In kernel form, my message has been this:

1. To view the Bible as literature is not a suspect modern idea, nor does it need to imply theological liberalism. The idea of the Bible as literature began with the writers of the Bible, who display literary qualities in their writings and who refer with technical precision to a wide range of literary genres such as psalm, proverb, parable, apocalypse, and many more.

2. Although fiction is a common trait of literature, it is not an essential feature of it. A work of literature can be replete with literary technique and artifice while remaining historically factual.

3. To approach the Bible as literature need not be characterized by viewing the Bible *only* as literature, any more than reading it as history requires us to see only the history of the Bible.

4. When we see literary qualities in the Bible, we are not attempting to bring the Bible down to the level of ordinary literature; it is simply an objective statement about the inherent nature of the Bible. The Bible can be trusted to reveal its extraordinary qualities if we approach it with ordinary methods of literary analysis.

To sum up, it would be tragic if we allowed ourselves to be deprived of literary methods of analyzing the Bible by claims that are fallacies.

What, then, does it mean to approach the Bible as literature? A literary study of the Bible should begin where any other approach begins—by accepting as true all that the biblical writers claim about their book. These claims include its inspiration and superintendence by God, its infallibility, its historical truthfulness, its unique power to infiltrate people's lives, and its supreme authority.

With that as a foundation, a literary approach to the Bible is characterized by the following traits:

1. An acknowledgement that the Bible comes to us in a predominantly literary format. In the words of C. S. Lewis, "There is a . . . sense in which the Bible, since it is after all literature, cannot properly be read except as literature; and the different parts of it as the different sorts

of literature they are."[1] The overall format of the Bible is that of an anthology of literature.

2. In keeping with that, a literary approach identifies the genres and other literary forms of the Bible and analyzes individual texts in keeping with those forms. An awareness of literary genres and forms programs how we analyze a biblical text and opens doors into a text that would otherwise remain closed.

3. A literary approach begins with the premise that a work of literature embodies universal human experience. Such truthfulness to human experience is complementary to the tendency of traditional approaches to the Bible to mainly see ideas in it. A literary approach corrects a commonly held fallacy that the Bible is a theology book with proof texts attached.

4. A literary approach to the Bible is ready to grant value to the biblical authors' skill with language and literary technique, seeing these as an added avenue to our enjoyment of the Bible.

5. A literary approach to the Bible takes its humble place alongside the two other main approaches—the theological and the historical. These three domains are established by the biblical writers themselves, who usually combine all three elements in their writings. However, in terms of space, the Bible is a predominantly literary book. Usually the historical and theological material is packaged in literary form.

These traits and methods of literary analysis govern the content of my series of guided studies to the genres of the Bible.

---

1   *Reflections on the Psalms* (New York: Harcourt, Brace & World, 1958), 3.

Although individual books in my series are organized by the leading literary genres that appear in the Bible, I need to highlight that all of these genres have certain traits in common. Literature itself, en masse, makes up a homogenous whole. In fact, we can speak of *literature as a genre* (the title of the opening chapter of a book titled *Kinds of Literature*). The traits that make up literature as a genre will simply be assumed in the volumes in this series. They include the following: universal, recognizable human experience concretely embodied as the subject matter; the packaging of this subject matter in distinctly literary genres; the authors' use of special resources of language that set their writing apart from everyday expository discourse; and stylistic excellence and other forms of artistry that are part of the beauty of a work of literature.

What are the advantages that come from applying the methods of literary analysis? In brief, they are as follows: an improved method of interacting with biblical texts in terms of the type of writing that they are; doing justice to the specificity of texts (again because the approach is tailored to the genres of a text); ability to see unifying patterns in a text; relating texts to everyday human experience; and enjoyment of the artistic skill of biblical authors.

Summary

A book needs to be read in keeping with its author's intention. We can see from the Bible itself that it is a thoroughly literary book. God superintended its authors to write a very (though not wholly) literary book. To pay adequate attention to the literary qualities of the Bible not only helps to unlock the meanings of the Bible but also honors the literary intentions of its authors. Surely biblical authors regarded everything that they put into their writing as important. We also need to regard those things as important.

Introduction

What Is Biblical Poetry?
And Why It Is Good for You

Next to narrative, poetry is the largest literary genre in the Bible. We cannot avoid it if we tried. Yet many Bible readers minimize their contact with the poetry of the Bible, and many who read it regularly feel uneasy with it. They read it more as a duty than a delight. Most preachers rarely preach from the poetry of the Bible. These considerations lead to the conclusion that the poetry of the Bible is experienced by most Bible readers as a problem requiring a solution. This guided study to the poetry of the Bible aims to open a doorway to biblical poetry. If it achieves its goal, you may find that the poetry of the Bible will become your favorite part of it.

Biblical Poetry as a Problem Genre

Much is to be gained by giving people's misgivings about poetry an airing. Once we have acknowledged the perceived obstacles to reading biblical poetry, we are in a position to address them and solve the problems. This unit of the chapter will lay the allegations out to view; the next unit will show that the perceived difficulties have good solutions. I have phrased the difficulties as *reasons not to immerse oneself in the poetry of the Bible.*

Reason #1: poetry is too difficult to understand. Even though not all biblical poetry is equally difficult, most of it requires more analytic skill than ordinary people possess (says the person who does not value poetry highly). Here is a specimen of the difficulty:

> My soul is in the midst of lions;
>   I lie down amid fiery beasts—
> the children of man, whose teeth are spears and arrows,
>   whose tongues are sharp swords. (Ps. 57:4)

No one's soul is in the midst of lions, and there is no such thing as fiery beasts. Similarly, no one's teeth are spears and arrows, nor are their tongues sharp swords. Ordinary people simply do not operate on this wave length.

Reason #2: poetry is optional in a person's life, not a necessity for everyone. Given the difficulty of poetry as a form of communication, some people regard it as optional reading and a matter of personal preference. People who love poetry and have an aptitude for it are free to choose it, say the skeptics. Those who do not have the aptitude for it should feel no obligation to burden themselves with it, and they should not feel guilty about leaving poetry for people who relish it.

Alternatively, even if people feel obligated to have *some* contact with biblical poetry, they are content to receive a vague feeling of elevation or peace from reading a psalm. They need not go to the effort of understanding a psalm in detail.

Reason #3: poetry is an unnatural form of discourse and therefore does not appeal to ordinary people. Prose is the normal form of communication, while poetry is an unnatural form. Just consider the following specimen:

I will greatly rejoice in the LORD;
    my soul shall exult in my God,
for he has clothed me with the garments of salvation;
    he has covered me with the robe of righteousness.
           (Isa. 61:10a)

In ordinary discourse we do not say everything twice the way the poet does here. In real life we do not wear garments of salvation or a robe of righteousness. Any form of writing that deviates this far from the ordinary way of expressing ourselves is an unnatural form of writing.

Reason #4: poetry is not worth the effort that it takes to master it. In view of all that has been said above, poetry is more of a liability than an asset. There is plenty of other material in the Bible to keep us occupied and edified.

Even people who do not subscribe to the foregoing reasons for not mastering the poetry of the Bible feel *some* degree of initial sympathy with the statements. It is helpful to see the case against poetry because it enables us to clarify what is true about biblical poetry.

Why Poetry Is Good for You

Despite an element of truthfulness in the objections to poetry, to accept them as a final verdict on biblical poetry will mislead us. The purpose of this unit of the chapter is to challenge the viewpoints expressed above.

Consideration #1: exactly how difficult is biblical poetry? All literary genres (such as stories or epistles) provide us with a continuum in regard to difficulty. Stories can be simple or complicated. A passage in an epistle might be easy to read, but it is just as often hard to piece together and understand.

We can see the same principle with poetry. The passages quoted above are on the more difficult half of the continuum, with their references to teeth like arrows and a robe of righteousness. But a passage like the following is on the easier half of the poetic continuum:

> The LORD is good,
>> a stronghold in the day of trouble;
> he knows those who take refuge in him. (Nahum 1:7)

We recognize this as poetry rather than prose, and as partly figurative instead of literal, but it is no more taxing on us than normal discourse.

In regard to the alleged difficulty of poetry, therefore, we need to be careful not to concede too much. Some poetry is decidedly difficult, but almost always a passage of difficult poetry will be immediately balanced by easier material. We also need to be forthright about the fact that the Bible is not an easy book to read but a difficult one. I will speak personally in saying that most times when I read a passage for daily devotions there is much that challenges me and quite a lot that I find perplexing. I regularly find myself consulting the notes of a study Bible to satisfy my questions about a passage, even in devotional reading.

Biblical poetry is within the reach of any dedicated reader who makes a good faith effort to understand it. The more we know about how poetry works, the easier we will find it to read biblical poetry with understanding and enjoyment. This guided study is designed to equip you to be a competent reader and teacher of biblical poetry.

Consideration #2: why biblical poetry is not optional but required. If we ask how we know that God intends for us to understand and enjoy poetry, the answer is that approximately a third of the Bible is poetic in form. Poetry is literally everywhere in the Bible. For starters, we can think of whole books that are wholly or largely poetic in format: Psalms, Proverbs, Song of Solomon, and Job. Additionally, vast parts of most of the Old Testament prophetic books are poetic. Then we need to add that the books of Ecclesiastes and Revelation, though mainly printed as prose, are actually poetic in technique.

Those are the obvious places where we find poetry in the Bible. But imagery and figurative language abound in parts of the Bible that we do not regard as poetry. The discourses and conversations of Jesus are an example: "I am the light of the world" (John 8:12 and 9:5); "you are the salt of the earth" (Matt. 5:13). Poetic language is also interspersed throughout the New Testament epistles: "at one time you were darkness, but now you are light in the Lord. Walk as children of light" (Eph. 5:8).

The conclusion is obvious: so much of the Bible consists of poetry that it is unthinkable to regard biblical poetry as optional in our reading diet and our menu of passages for Bible teaching. It is instructive to ponder Paul's claim that Christians are God's poem: "For we are his workmanship [Greek *poeima*, from which we get our word *poem*], created in Christ Jesus for good works" (Eph. 2:10).

Consideration #3: exactly how unnatural is poetry? Is poetry an unnatural form of discourse? The answer is yes and no.

We can begin with how poetry is more natural than we may think. Everyone uses figurative language during the course of a typical day. We speak of road hogs, game changers, cliff hangers, and nightmare tests, even though we know that none of these is literally true. No one has ever literally juggled a schedule or killed time, but we keep speaking in these terms anyway. We do so because it seems like a natural way to name the experiences that are in view.

Additionally, it is an interesting fact of literary history that in most ancient cultures, poetry preceded prose as an accomplished form of expression. How could that be if prose is the natural form of expression and poetry an unnatural form? We wrongly think that prose is a natural medium; it is actually a sophisticated form of expression. In everyday situations we do not speak prose (complete sentences with a subject and predicate). We speak an associative discourse comprised of single words and phrases, disjointed and incomplete sentence fragments, and arrangement by stream of consciousness instead of formal syntax (sentence structure). Prose is everyday discourse on its best behavior.

But in other ways it is true that poetry is an unnatural or extraordinary form of speaking—something out of the routine and not the way people usually express themselves. So much the better. Poetry has a quality that J. R. R. Tolkien ascribed to fantasy and fairy tales: "arresting strangeness." Poetry can overcome the cliché effect of ordinary discourse. It startles us with its unusualness and forces us to analyze a statement when ordinary ways of stating the same content are overly familiar. A poem is like a still-life painting of a bowl of fruit: it compels our attention when the same scene in real life makes little or no impact on us.

Consideration #4: biblical poetry is definitely worth the effort of mastering it. There is a religious side to this claim and a literary side. The religious side is that God entrusted a third of the Bible—his revelation of himself and his ways—to poetry. No one wishes to carry a Bible with a third of its pages removed. We would not even want the Psalms to be missing.

Quite apart from this religious argument, poetry offers literary rewards that are unique to it. Of course the same is true of other literary genres. No other form of writing is an adequate substitute for poetry. Poetry combines truth and beauty in a higher concentration than other genres. For anyone who remains skeptical of this claim, I extend an invitation to undertake the journey with me that I will conduct in the rest of this guided study.

What Is Poetry?

Thus far I have assumed that we are all on the same page regarding what poetry is, but I need to sharpen the focus here at the end of the chapter.

It is possible to be so struck by the unusualness of poetry that we overlook that it belongs to the overall genre known as literature. At this level, poetry possesses all of the usual qualities of literature. Its subject is human experience, concretely rendered. It is truthful to human experience and life. It possesses artistry that is self-rewarding as a form of beauty. It is entertaining as well as edifying.

What, then, sets poetry apart from other literary genres such as stories, visions, and letters? It is a more concentrated form of expression. A poet packs more meaning into a line than other authors typically do. Even the sentences of poetry are more compressed, as seen by the fact that poetic lines do not run all the way to the right margin of a page. A poetic image or figure of speech usually embodies multiple meanings. C. S. Lewis used the phrase "line by line deliciousness" to name this quality of compression that poetry possesses.

If poetry is more concentrated than ordinary discourse, it is also more consciously and abundantly artistic. There is simply more to notice and say about the organization and technique in a typical poem than in a typical story or epistle. Consequently, we more readily ascribe the aesthetic quality of beauty to a poem than we do to other genres. We definitely need to accept the premise that beauty of expression is an important part of every poem, including the poems of the Bible.

Summary

It is unwise either to exaggerate or understate the difference of poetry from other forms of discourse. The most obvious feature of poetry is that it is not how we ordinarily speak. Poets have a way with words that ordinary people only rarely possess. Far from being a mark against poetry, it highlights the way in which poetry performs a function in the human economy and the spiritual life that is unique. Additionally, the departure of poetry from ordinary discourse is not as great as it initially seems. Mastering this unusual form of communication is within the reach of anyone who makes a genuine effort.

PART 1

The Language Poets Use

First Things First

The Primacy of the Image

Before we explore the subject of *poems* (compositions), we need to understand *poetry*. Poetry is the material out of which poems are made. It is like the wood out of which a table is made. First there is wood, and then the table is fashioned out of it. This chapter and the next two deal with poetry as a type of language. A literary scholar once entitled a book introducing readers to poetry *The Language Poets Use*.[2] That is the subject of the first three chapters of this book. The phrase "the poetic idiom" is also a common way of designating poetic language.

Success in dealing with the poetry of the Bible rests especially on three principles. These constitute chapters 1–3 of this guided study. They are arranged in a hierarchy of importance, starting with the primacy of the image in poetry.

---

2   Winifred Nowottny, *The Language Poets Use*, 5th ed. (New York: Bloomsbury Academic, 2000).

Poetry as a Language of Images

The broadest possible thing that we can say about poetry is that it consists of a language of images. An image is any word that names a concrete thing or action. Running and sleeping are images that name a physical action. A tree planted by streams of water is an image in the form of a physical thing. Loosely speaking, anything we can visualize is an image. We can also profitably think of a poetic image as presenting us with a picture. But an image can be a sound or touch, too.

The totality of images in a poem is called *imagery*. This word is actually a catch-all term that is also used to name *a pattern of images* in a poem. Thus Psalm 1 uses the imagery of the path or way at the beginning and end of the poem, and nature and harvest imagery in the middle. Although literary scholars would not ordinarily use the word "image" to name abstractions like good and evil, they would feel comfortable speaking of the imagery of good and evil in Psalm 1.

The conclusion to be drawn from the preceding two paragraphs is that the terms "image" and "imagery" are flexible terms that can be used somewhat loosely. The next chapter will explore metaphor and simile as figures of speech, but no literary scholar would be bent out of shape if you refer to a metaphor or simile as an image. The important thing is to perform the right interpretive activities with images, metaphors, and similes.

This chapter is devoted to the idea that the primary unit of poetry is the image, as defined above. One way to prove the principle of the primacy of the image in poetry is to draw up two lists that name the substance or content that we find when we read the Old Testament book of Psalms. Anyone familiar with the Psalms would acknowledge that we find the following topics repeatedly in the Psalms:

- godliness
- mercy
- forgiveness
- goodness
- evil
- providence
- worship
- depression

The most obvious feature of this list is that the words name abstractions and topics. We would not call it a list of images (words naming a concrete action or thing).

Here is a second, equally accurate list of what we find in the Psalms:

- honey (Ps. 19:10)
- thunder (Ps. 29:3)
- razor (Ps. 52:2)
- broken arm (Ps. 37:17)
- grass (Ps. 147:8)
- bread (Ps. 127:2)

This is quite a different list from the first one, and it is instructive to compare the two lists to each other.

When we do so, we end up with a series of contrasts. The first list is abstract, and the second one is concrete (a language of images). The first list strikes us as religious in nature (or at least having obvious religious implications), while the second one seems religiously neutral and in that sense secular rather than spiritual or religious.

Would we say that the second list is what the psalms are about? We would not say that. The first list is what the psalms are about. Yet the poets overwhelmingly speak the vocabulary of the second list (a language of images). The poet in Psalm 23 uses the imagery of sheep and shepherd, but his subject is God's providence.

In view of the foregoing, we can see that most poetry is based on a principle of *indirection*. The poet uses a language of images as a way of writing about something else. American poet Robert Frost helpfully spoke of poetry as saying one thing and meaning another.

Poets predominantly speak a language of images, but this does not rule out the possibility of something that literary scholars call *the poetry of direct statement*. While most poetry contains some inclusion of direct statement or abstraction, there is probably more direct statement and abstraction in the poetry of the Bible (not counting the Song of Solomon) than in poetry generally. The following is an example of the intermixture of direct statement and imagery in a passage of biblical poetry:

> For the LORD God is a sun and shield [images];
>> the LORD bestows favor and honor [direct statement].
> No good thing does he withhold [direct statement]
>> from those who walk uprightly [images]. (Ps. 84:11)

We can say of poets that they usually think and feel in images. As readers of poetry, we need to follow the contour that poets lay down and also think and feel in images.

What Images Require of Us as Readers

What activities do the images of poetry require of us as readers? The first is to experience the images as concretely and vividly as possible. We need to picture what the poet pictures for us by means of words. We need to hear and smell and touch what the poet embodies in images. When we teach biblical poetry, we should not scorn anything that will make the images come alive in our students' imaginations. We should carry our visual aids to class, no matter how rudimentary. Students *want* to experience poetic images as images and will be responsive to any help we give.

In addition to this *descriptive level* (experiencing the image as an image), there are several *interpretive* activities in which we need to engage. I am sure that it will surprise some of my readers to think of interpreting what I call the *straight image* (as distinct from metaphor and simile, which compare one thing to another). But even the straight image requires interpretation.

Three specific types of interpretation might be noted: we need to identify the connotations of the image in the context of the poem; we need to name the emotions that are evoked by the image; and we need to explore the logic of the image in the context of the poem. All three of these will be explored below. We should note that each of the three categories needs to be explored when it is relevant for a given image. If one or more of the categories do not apply, we obviously need not concern ourselves with them.

Connotations of Images

Words have two types of meanings. One is the *denotation*—what might be called the dictionary definition. Such a definition is largely objective. It does not evoke subjective feelings or attitudes. The other type of meaning consists of *connotations*. Connotations are feelings, attitudes, and associations that gather around a word or image. In regard to poetry, these connotations are often present because of their placement in a specific poem or passage. We can say emphatically that connotations of words are much more prevalent in poems than in the ordinary circumstances of life.

We can use the word "home" as an illustration. The dictionary definition of home is "the place where a person lives." That definition is objective and stripped of subjective associations. By contrast, the connotations of the word "home" are multiple and highly charged: security, safety, comfort, family, a sense of belonging, retreat from the wear and tear of life in the public arena.

To see how this applies to poetry, we can explore the images in the following passage. The passage comes from the book of Job (24:2–3), and the context is Job's portrait of how the wicked exploit and oppress the poor and helpless:

> Some move landmarks;
>> they seize flocks and pasture them.
> They drive away the donkey of the fatherless;
>> they take the widow's ox for a pledge.

As we turn to exploration of the individual images, we should remind ourselves that in another context the connotations might be different. Here is an anatomy of the connotations of the images in the quoted passage:

- *Moving landmarks.* A landmark is a marker that identifies the legal boundary of someone's property. It is customarily a cornerstone placed securely in the ground in a location that is determined by a surveyor. It is legally binding. Once determined, a landmark needs to be kept in place as a permanent marker that protects an owner's rights. To "move landmarks" has connotations of dishonesty, disregard for property rights, stealing, and undermining a basic foundation of civilization.

- *Seizing flocks and pasturing them.* We might start with the connotations of flocks and pastures. They belong to the idealized world of pastoral literature; in fact, they are a kind of shorthand for all that is most treasured in pastoral literature and in the real-life world of shepherds and shepherding. A shepherd's flock is his livelihood, and pastures are an image of abundance and economic sustenance. To "seize flocks" connotes destroying someone's livelihood by removing the means of production, and to "pasture" the stolen flocks is an implied picture of the thief incorporating them into his own possessions.

- *Drive away the donkey of the fatherless.* As the litany of oppressive acts continues to unfold, we remain in a farming world of animals. Like flocks, donkeys would have been a staple of life. To "drive away the donkey" probably connotes (as in the preceding verse) a powerful bully simply confiscating someone else's property. But the connotations explode when the victim of this theft turns out to be "the fatherless." Perhaps no other groups carry deeper connotations of poverty and helplessness in the Old Testament than the fatherless (orphans) and widows. What would be an ordinary outrage becomes greatly intensified when it happens to the fatherless.

- *Taking the widow's ox.* The ox was (once again) an animal of economic and farming importance. It was the ancient equivalent of a tractor. One could not farm without an ox to pull the plow and carry burdens. The connotations of "widow" are helplessness, vulnerability, the weakest of the weak in terms of being able to provide daily security.

Analysis of this type is not an option if we wish to understand what poetic images communicate; it is a necessity.

Interpreting the Affective Level of Poetic Images

Images not only embody connotations; they also frequently awaken emotions. Poetry is a more affective (emotional) type of discourse than ordinary expository discourse. Naming the feelings that are evoked by an image is a genuine and important type of literary commentary on a poem. We should not shrink from such naming of feelings simply because it strikes some people as simpleminded. Our experience of poetry and teaching of it are richer if we are attuned to the feelings that are elicited by poetic images. The following passage (Ps. 59:14–15) is David's poetic remembrance of what it was like "when Saul sent men to watch his house in order to kill him" (from the headnote):

> Each evening they come back,
> > howling like dogs
> > and prowling about the city.
> They wander about for food
> > and growl if they do not get their fill.

What feelings do these images evoke? The answers include fear, repulsion, helplessness, confinement, terror, disgust, and outrage over being confined by wild dogs surrounding the house.

Interpreting the Logic of Images

In addition to analyzing the connotations and feelings evoked by poetic images, we need to explore their logic. We will revisit this subject of logic in the next chapter when we look at metaphor and simile. But even the straight image can be analyzed for its logic.

Modern poet Stephen Spender wrote an essay entitled "The Making of a Poem." In it he claimed that "the terrifying challenge" facing a poet is, "Can I think out the logic of images?" Logic means suitability, connection, fittingness, or correlation. Applied to poetic imagery, it means that we need to explore the connection between a given image and the subject of the poem or passage. A good question to ask in this regard is, Why this image for this poem or passage? What is the logic of it? Analyzing this angle yields a lot of insight into a poem.

The following passage is a portrait drawn by the prophet Amos about the lifestyle of the complacent wealthy class of his day (Amos 6:4, 6):

Woe to those who lie on beds of ivory
    and stretch themselves out on their couches,
and eat lambs from the flock
    and calves from the midst of the stall . . . ,
who drink wine in bowls
    and anoint themselves with the finest oils.

The logic at work in the individual images works out something like the following:

- *Body posture.* The images that fit into this pattern are lying and stretching out. Why did the poet to choose images of body posture? The logic is multiple. On a physical level, lying down and stretching out are a picture of laziness, lack of effort, taking the easy way out. Amos is portraying the original couch potatoes. But Amos is also tapping into a technique of poets through the ages of using body parts and posture to symbolize a spiritual state of soul. Amos is painting a portrait of the spiritually complacent, smug, conceited, and arrogant.
- *Furniture.* In painting his character sketch, Amos includes two images of furniture—"beds of ivory" and "couches." We can take both of these to be pieces of expensive and ostentatious furniture. What is the logic of including furniture in the portrait? The answer is that Amos is writing about the wealthy class of his day. Nothing could take us to the heart of such influence more quickly than two references to the expensive furniture that these people own.

- *Wine by the bowl full.* The purpose of the passage is to paint a picture of a lifestyle and the people who live it. Social drinking is an important part of the lifestyle of the wealthy. That is why Amos brings the detail into his portrait. But there is an additional nuance of logic: these social drinkers (or solitary drinkers at home in the afternoon) drink wine *in bowls*. Even if the idea is not excess to the point of intoxication, the image of the bowl at least adds the twist of a high level of consumption. The overall logic of the portrait that Amos paints is that of self-indulgence on a grand scale, made possible by the affluence of the people involved. Wine by the bowl fulls fits that logic.
- *Cosmetics.* The final image in the quoted passage takes us to the realm of cosmetics in the specific form of skin lotions. Contemporary images of advertisements might well flood our imagination, and I think particularly of an advertisement that features the slogan "every inch Clinique" (the latter being the brand name). The logic of the image is that it conveys a sense of pampering oneself and being preoccupied with appearance and physical comfort. The overall logic of the portrait is that of extreme self-indulgence by the wealthy. In working this out, it would not suit the logic of the situation to speak only of "oils." Amos needed the added dimension of "the finest oils."

The foregoing analysis has shown two things. One is that when poets choose their images they have a game plan in mind based on the logic of their images (how the images correlate with the content of a passage). Secondly, it is obvious that exploring the logic of images is a very fruitful avenue to seeing how a passage of poetry gains its effects and communicates its meanings.

LEARNING BY DOING

The subject of this chapter is not metaphor, simile, and other complex figures of speech. Instead it covers what might be called "the straight image." Even the straight image requires analysis if we wish to garner all the meanings of a poem. The foregoing section of theory has set forth a fourfold grid for analysis, as follows:

- Experiencing the literal, physical properties of the image (the image as an image).
- Identifying the connotations of an image.
- Naming the feelings evoked by an image.
- Exploring the logic of an image—its relevance to the subject of the passage.

In each case, a given item on the grid needs to be relevant before we can explore it; if an image does not lend itself to one or more items on the grid, we can pass right over it.

In the units above the individual items on the grid were treated individually. When we analyze a poem, we progress through the poem image by image, verse by verse. With experience, we develop a knack for sensing which of the considerations comes into play with a given image. We always need to relieve the image as a literal phenomenon, but with connotations, emotions, and logic, we activate only the items that are helpful for a given image. The overall process that encompasses the entire grid can be thought of as *unpacking the meanings of an image.*

The following passage (Micah 4:1–5) describes God's rule in the world (either in history or in the age to come). The overall logic of the passage is to assert and extol that rule. It is possible to apply the grid outlined above to the images of the passage.

¹It shall come to pass in the latter days
> that the mountain of the house of the LORD
shall be established as the highest of the mountains,
> and it shall be lifted up above the hills;
and peoples shall flow to it,
> ²and many nations shall come, and say:
"Come, let us go up to the mountain of the LORD,
> to the house of the God of Jacob,
that he may teach us his ways
> and that we may walk in his paths."
For out of Zion shall go forth the law,
> and the word of the LORD from Jerusalem.
³He shall judge between many peoples,
> and shall decide for strong nations far away;
and they shall beat their swords into plowshares,
> and their spears into pruning hooks;
nation shall not lift up sword against nation,
> neither shall they learn war anymore;
⁴but they shall sit every man under his vine and under his fig tree,
> and no one shall make them afraid,
> for the mouth of the LORD of hosts has spoken.
⁵For all the peoples walk
> each in the name of its god,
but we will walk in the name of the LORD our God
> forever and ever.

Final Thoughts on the Primacy of the Image in Poetry

The formula "the primacy of the image in poetry" was carefully chosen. Imagery is primary in poetry in the sense that it is the most prevalent thing that we encounter when we read poetry. But aren't metaphor and simile and other figures of speech equally dominant? The answer is yes, but most other figures of speech, and certainly all metaphors and similes, are images first of all. Before A is compared to B in a metaphoric statement, A needs to exist in its own right as an image.

We might wonder why poets write in a language of images. The answer is that images are a way of thinking before they are a way of writing. This is not to imply that in the ordinary daily routine poets think only in images. It is a way of saying that for purposes of composition, a poet cannot write in images without first thinking and imagining in images.

All of us, and not only poets, formulate our understanding of life partly in terms of ideas and abstractions, but also partly in terms of images and concretions. This is well illustrated in the discourse methods of Jesus. When Jesus was asked, "And who is my neighbor?" (Luke 10:29), the situation was tailor-made for a dictionary definition: "your neighbor is anyone in need who crosses your path." Jesus did not enter that door. Instead he told the story of the Good Samaritan in which everything is embodied in images.

The importance of logic has been obvious in this chapter. Two additional things need to be said about it. The words "correlation" and "correlative" are good synonyms for logic. How does a poet embody feelings in words? Talking directly about emotions does not take the poet very far. Instead the poet thinks of images that *correlate with* and *evoke* the desired feelings. The images might seem to be far removed from the actual subject of a poem, but the poet uses them to *evoke a feeling* by indirect means.

Second, while the focus of this chapter has fallen on the logic of individual images, it is also useful to our understanding of a poem to state the overall logic of the poem. The overall logic explains why the poet chose the individual images that we find in a poem. For example, in Psalm 91 (a psalm that celebrates God's protection of those who trust in him), the overall logic is to point to heightened pictures of danger and correspondingly heightened pictures of protection. This overall logic explains why we find images of warfare and trapping and sunstroke and traveling.

Summary

Poets think and imagine in images, and so must we as readers of poetry. Analyzing poetic images in terms of literal properties, connotations, feelings, and logic is an avenue to finding what is present in a poem. It is actually a way of going through the process of composition that the poet experienced when inventing the poem in the first place. In fact, it is a useful strategy to imagine oneself composing the poem, going through the same steps that the poet went through.

How Is A Like B?

The Use of Metaphor and Simile

While the image is the foundational element of poetry, and the most pervasive in poetry, from the time of Aristotle experts in poetry have agreed that the skill that distinguishes poets as masters of their craft is the gift for inventing metaphors and similes. The knack for seeing resemblances is, even more than the ability to think in images, the "qualifying exam" for great poets. Aristotle said that the gift of metaphor is "the greatest thing by far" for a poet.

We need to define terms here at the outset of the chapter. A metaphor is an *implied* assertion of correspondence. A simile is an *explicit* assertion of correspondence that uses the formula "like" or "as." The statement "you are all children of light" (1 Thess. 5:5) is a metaphor because it implies a comparison between how believers live and light. The statement that "the path of the righteous is like the light of dawn" (Prov. 4:18) is a simile because it uses the formula "like."

In regard to metaphor, even though many metaphors use a form of the verb "is" (e.g., "the LORD is my shepherd"), this is not a requirement for calling an implied comparison a metaphor. A metaphor can be more latent or subtle than an "is" statement, and in such instances we may need to ferret out the fact that we are dealing with a metaphor. For example, when the poet says that "the snares of death encompassed me" (Ps. 116:3), we assimilate the statement as a metaphor, even though there is no "am" or "is" verb. Generally speaking, if a statement is not literally true, that is often an invitation to regard it as a metaphor, or *metaphoric*.

We should also note the following matter of terminology. Even though there are differences between a metaphor and a simile, what they share is even more important than the differences. What they share is the principle of *comparison or correspondence*. They simply differ in how they assert that correspondence. For this reason, when literary scholars discuss the element of comparison in metaphor and simile, they frequently speak only of metaphor, on the understanding that what they assert extends to similes as well.

A Primer on Metaphor and Simile

As already hinted, metaphor and simile hold an honored place in the sphere of poetry. Some of the first principles regarding metaphor and simile are things they share with the poetic image (as covered in the preceding chapter), but there are other dimensions that belong just to them. The following are seven important things to know about metaphor and simile.

1. The essence of a metaphor or simile is the principle of correspondence. Another term by which we can name this is the word "*analogy*." In a metaphor or simile, one thing is *compared* to another similar thing. Aristotle's formulation was that "to make good metaphors implies an eye for resemblances." If we ask why poets desire to use comparisons as a way of expressing their content, one

answer is that they see the effectiveness of using one area of human experience to illuminate or shed light on another area of human experience. There can be no doubt that poets have a particular knack for doing this, so that we can speak of metaphor and simile being a way of thinking before they are a mode of expression.

2. Metaphor and simile are bifocal statements. They require us to have two things in view—the actual subject of a passage or poem and the other thing to which that subject is compared. Or we could reverse that: in reading or hearing a metaphor, we first encounter the thing to which the subject is being compared, and then we are aware that the actual subject of the statement is something else.

3. Through the ages, literary critics have struggled to find good terms for the two halves of the comparison for both metaphors and similes. This guide will simply use the formulas *level A* and *level B* for the two halves. Level A is the literal image—the thing to which the subject is being compared. Level B is the actual subject of the utterance. In the statement "you are the salt of the earth" (Matt. 5:13), salt (the literal reference) is level A, and those who follow Christ (the actual subject of the utterance) is level B. In the preceding chapter on the primacy of the image in poetry, we observed in passing that a metaphor or simile is an image first (level A) and then becomes a metaphor or simile when the element of comparison is added to the mix.

4. All of this talk about level A and level B will make more sense if we add the following methodology for interpreting a metaphor or simile. The essential interpretive activity of metaphor and simile required of us is highlighted by the

word "metaphor." Our English word "metaphor" is based on two Greek words—*meta* and *pherein*. The first word means "over," and the second means "to carry." The task of interpreting a metaphor or simile consists of *carrying over* the meaning from level A to level B. Here is an example: "The vineyard of the LORD of hosts / is the house of Israel" (Isa. 5:7). There are actually two metaphors here— the vineyard and the house. Those two images are level A. Having let the meanings of those two images sink into our minds, and having experienced them as images, we need to "carry over" those meanings to the actual subject of the passage—the people of Israel (and by extension the believing community everywhere).

5. Metaphor and simile are a form of logic. They can be studied (and often are) in logic courses. The accuracy of a metaphor or simile can be tested by ordinary tests of logical accuracy. To do so requires us to think about the comparison that the poet has claimed to be true. It requires reasoning, leisurely meditation, and analysis.

6. Metaphor and simile are based on a principle of *indirection*. They compare the subject of the moment to something else that it is literally *not*. American poet Robert Frost went so far as to say that metaphor and simile are a way of "saying one thing and meaning another." The poet *says* that "the name of the LORD is a strong tower" (Prov. 18:10); he *means* that God protects those who seek him.

7. In view of the foregoing, we need to acknowledge that metaphor and simile are a poet's invitation to us to *discover the meaning*. The poet simply asserts a correspondence between two things; it is left to us to determine *how* A is like B. This is a big responsibility for the reader. There

is of course always a possibility of misinterpreting how A is like B. It is obviously a risk that biblical poets and the God who superintended what they wrote, thought worth taking.

Psalm 23 as a Test Case

The subject of the first three chapters of this guided study is not poems but poetry—the language poets use (also called *the poetic idiom*). There has been no premium on paying attention to entire poems. To illustrate the dynamics of how to assimilate metaphors and similes, therefore, I will take individual verses from Psalm 23 and look at them by themselves.

Psalm 23 is the best possible poem with which to illustrate how metaphors and similes work. For starters, Psalm 23 is the greatest poem of all time (the verdict of the author of this guide). More importantly, Psalm 23 is built around a controlling image or controlling metaphor. This means that the frame of reference— the shepherd's provision for his sheep during the course of a typical day—is constant from start to finish. All the way through the poem, level A consists of what a good shepherd does for his sheep. Level B is also constant: the provisions that God extends to those who follow him. We can thus do with the entire poem what we ordinarily do for individual metaphors or similes.

To anticipate, a metaphor or simile imposes a double obligation on a reader and interpreter. First we need to experience the image—level A—as fully as possible. Then we need to carry over the meaning(s) to level B (the actual subject of the poem). Almost always, we will find multiple meanings in the initial image (applying virtually everything covered in the preceding chapter on imagery) that need to be carried over to level B. The following demonstration will take selected images from Psalm 23.

- *The LORD is my shepherd; I shall not want.* (v. 1). This
  line introduces the controlling metaphor of the sheep-
  shepherd relationship. To assimilate the image at level
  A, we need to go beyond the poem and reconstruct what
  conditions of shepherding were like in ancient Palestine
  (and in some places to this very day). Sheep were not
  fenced in and could not fend for themselves. They
  depended for their life on their shepherd's ability to lead
  them from the overnight sheepfold to places of grazing
  and drinking. Palestine has a rocky and treacherous
  terrain, and it is totally subject to drought for much of
  the year. In short, it is a picture of total dependence.
  If that is what is true at level A of the image, that is
  what we carry over to level B—an assertion of how God
  provides for the needs of those who follow him. If sheep
  are totally dependent on their shepherd, so are people in
  relation to God.
- *He makes me lie down in green pastures. / He leads me beside
  still waters* (v. 2). Again we need the help of context in
  order to understand the literal picture. Left to your own
  designs, we would think that the provision being described
  is food and water for the sheep. After all, pastures are where
  sheep graze and streams are where they drink. The daily
  routine of shepherds in Palestine was to lead their sheep
  from the sheepfold early in the day to places of grazing
  and watering. When this was finished, the sheep would lie
  down in the middle of the day and rest for several hours in
  the best place that a shepherd could find for such rest (an
  oasis-like place would of course be best). (This is confirmed
  by Song of Solomon 1:7: "Tell me . . . / where you pasture
  your flock, / where you make it lie down at noon.") The
  literal picture is thus a picture of the sheep at rest in a

state of total contentment, with all their physical needs met. What categories of human experience are pictured by this pastoral scene of sheep at rest? When we carry over the meanings to a human level, we first of all end up with broad categories that we regularly experience—rest, refreshment, contentment, beauty, peace, freedom from anxiety, retreat. Anything that we can picture that is *like* sheep resting at midday is an accurate interpretation. Then we can move from broad categories to specific experiences of the past day or week or year.

- *He leads me in right paths* (v. 3, ESV footnote; NRSV main text). The literal picture at the level of a shepherd's provision for his sheep is leading the sheep on safe paths between the sheepfold and places of grazing and watering. There is an implied journey motif and guidance motif. A "right" path is a safe path. How does God guide his followers in a manner that is like the shepherd's guidance of sheep on safe paths? The carryovers are multiple (as they almost always are with metaphors and similes): God's moral law; the Bible as God's guidebook for life; the example and teachings of Christ; the indwelling presence of the Holy Spirit; circumstances of life; exhortations from godly people; the good influence of peers, parents, spouse, or child; and conscience. Biblical scholars often get nervous about the seeming subjectivity involved in finding carryovers. The answer is that this is simply how metaphor and simile work. We can trust the broader community of interpreters to weed out incorrect carryovers that we might make on our own.

- *Even though I walk through the valley of deep darkness, I fear no evil.* (v. 4, ESV footnote; NRSV, *darkest valley*). The imagery here continues the imagery of a journey on a path introduced in the preceding verse. The picture is that of a dangerous place in a sheep's pathway, a place where predators might lurk, and a dark and low place where sheep might be fearful. The picture combines two evocative archetypes (recurrent master images) of life and literature—darkness and a low valley, both of which have symbolic overtones. When we carry over the meanings from the level of sheep and shepherd (level A) to a human level, the list keeps expanding. What are the dark valleys of our life? Death, adversity, accident, loneliness, depression, breakup of relationships, moral temptation, doubt, sin, in fact any of the fearful experiences that come into our lives. Is that really how metaphor works? Yes—you need to take my word for it as coming from someone who has taught poetry for nearly half a century. But, we might protest, this process of "carrying over" looks like a simple process. Yes, it is a simple process and does not require a seminary education to perform. We might note in passing how marvelously compressed poetry is as a form of communication.

- *Your rod and staff comfort me* (v. 4). This provision of the shepherd is still part of the picture of sheep being led and protected as they travel along a potentially dangerous and fearful pathway during the routine course of the day. The shepherd's rod was the familiar crook, used for disciplining wandering sheep or reaching down into a gully and rescuing a sheep from it. The staff was more of a club for warding off attacking animals or getting the attention of a stubborn sheep. The combined picture is one of protection and rescue. It is easy to carry over those meanings to our own lives. When I teach Psalm 23 in class, I begin a series of autobiographical devotionals that I term "the rod and staff series." The series consists of stories of God's intervening providentially and notably in people's lives in such a way as to prevent a disaster or rescue someone when a disaster does happen. The experiences thus recounted usually fall into the categories of extreme providence or the miraculous (with the latter often occurring on the mission field).

The foregoing is more than enough to illustrate the process of experiencing and interpreting metaphors and similes. The next step is to apply the process on your own.

LEARNING BY DOING

Since the subject of this chapter (like the chapters that precede and follow it) is the language poets use, and not compositions made out of such poetic language, there is no need to ask for an explication of an entire poem. Instead the following material consists of a collection of promising examples of metaphors and similes. Your assignment is to (1) relive level A as fully as possible (getting the literal picture) and (2) carry over the meanings to level B (the actual subject of the passage) in whatever ways are accurate and relevant. We need to start with the literal properties of the image as it exists at level A.

Job commenting on his sufferings:
> God has cast me into the mire,
> and I have become like dust and ashes. (Job 30:19)

The poet describing the threat posed by his enemy:
> He is like a lion eager to tear,
> as a young lion lurking in ambush. (Ps. 17:12)

God's promise of a (promise of a coming age) coming golden age for his people (in its original setting, Old Testament Israel):

> I will be like the dew to Israel;
>> he shall blossom like the lily;
>>> he shall take root like the trees of Lebanon. (Hosea 14:5)

A passage of nature poetry that praises God's control of the forces of nature:

> He gives snow like wool;
>> he scatters frost like ashes. (Ps. 147:16)

A description of God's followers:

> We are his people, and the sheep of his pasture. (Ps. 100:3)

An exchange of compliments by a man and woman in love:

> As a lily among brambles,
>> so is my love among the young women.
> As an apple tree among the trees of the forest,
>> so is my beloved among the young men.
>> (Song of Solomon 2:2–3)

Lifestyle or pattern of living compared to walking down a path (an archetype that appears repeatedly in the Bible):

> Who forsake the paths of uprightness
>> to walk in the ways of darkness, . . .
> men whose paths are crooked,
>> and who are devious in their ways. (Prov. 2:13, 15)

On the essential quality of life lived by purely earthly values, without God at the center:

> Vapor of vapors, says the Preacher,
>> vapor of vapors! All is vapor. (Eccl. 1:2, ESV footnote)

How is life "under the sun" like a vapor?

Jesus' description of how to enter the kingdom of God:

> Enter by the narrow gate. For the gate is wide and the way is easy that leads to destruction. . . . For the gate is narrow and the way is hard that leads to life. (Matt. 7:13–14)

How is entering the kingdom like passing through a gate and walking down a pathway, and what are the meanings of a narrow gate and straight path as contrasted to a wide gate?

A description of God:

> The name of the LORD is a strong tower;
> the righteous man runs into it and is safe. (Prov. 18:10)

Final Thoughts on Metaphor and Simile in Biblical Poetry

I hope that my readers will have assimilated the foregoing material with a degree of surprise and discovery—and even relief. Poetry is sufficiently different from everyday discourse that it may well intimidate us at first. But once we get inside of metaphor and simile as forms of communication, they are essentially simple. How is A like B? Determining that is within reach of anyone who is willing to read at a meditative speed and engage in thought about what is read. When a given metaphor or simile is difficult, it is usually because level A—the literal image—belongs to the ancient rather than modern world, but the need to recover the original context extends to the whole Bible and is not a feature of poetry per se.

I can imagine some of my readers being skeptical that interpreting metaphors and similes is as simple as I have portrayed it. My response is that study Bibles and commentaries have let us down through sins of omission. Consider the following quotations from study Bibles in regard to a metaphor that occurs more than half a dozen times in the Psalms, namely, God's elevation of his people compared to raising up a horn (that is, the horn of an animal): "the term 'horn' scarcely needs comment, with its evident implications of strength;" "'horn' signifies might and power;" "figurative for granting victory or bestowing prosperity;" "'horn' here symbolizes strong one, that is, king."

These comments completely conceal the fact that the poet has given us a metaphor that requires us first to experience a literal image and then carry over the associations to a second level. It is no wonder that Bible readers are inexperienced in interpreting metaphors and similes. Additionally, bald statements about what the image of "raising up a horn" *means or signifies* makes the process of interpretation seem like something only biblical scholars can perform. The material that I have covered in this chapter is the common reader's friend and ally.

The logic of metaphor and simile is that they draw upon one area of human experience to illuminate another area. The various aspects of walking down a path really do highlight certain features of a person's life. Biblical interpreters who leapfrog over level A and tell us what level B means do not believe that the physical properties of walking down a path illuminate anything about a person's lifestyle. Level A is simply a vehicle for an idea, and perhaps even a distraction. We should not settle for this approach to the poetry of the Bible.

Summary

Next to the poetic image, comparison is the most prevalent aspect of the language poets' use. The specific form that this takes is the figures of speech called metaphor and simile. We can feel comfortable when dealing with metaphors and similes if we simply keep the basic paradigm in view. In metaphor and simile, A is compared to B. First we need to identify and experience level A as fully as possible. This requires that we take time to ponder the image. Then we need to carry over the meanings that we ascribed to the image to level B, which is the actual subject of the passage we are analyzing.

Make-Believe

Poetry and the Nonliteral

We have observed in the preceding two chapters that poets speak a language all their own. The staples of that language are imagery, metaphor, and simile. But we cannot read very far in biblical poetry before seeing that there is an abundance of other figures of speech beyond the "basic three." This chapter will identify the further menu of figurative language, along with the right methodology for assimilating and interpreting this menu.

The rubric under which I will discuss the figures of speech is the poets' love for the nonliteral. In fact, I would dare to assert that poets *prefer* the nonliteral. We might say that at the surface level of their poetry, poets are always playing a game of make-believe—telling us something that we know to be literally false. We can accurately speak of poetry as being inherently fictional and often fantastic.

When we say that, we are talking about the surface level of a poem. Poetry uses the nonliteral to tell us about things that really exist. The question is *how* poetry expresses that truth and reality.

The poet's task, at the surface level of discourse, can be placed under the formula "the making of unreality." The common formula *poetic license* is also a handy concept.

We have seen the impulse toward this making of unreality in the preceding two chapters. Much of the time the *straight image* is literal, but even with such imagery we noted a tendency toward indirection. That is, the images that the poet collected were designed to awaken an emotion as aroused by the images and are not what the poem is actually about.

With metaphor and simile, we take a big step toward something even more openly nonliteral. At a literal or grammatical level, a metaphor is always a fiction or "lie." It asserts something that we know is not literally true: "The LORD is my rock" (Ps. 18:2). Even though a simile is grammatically true (since it uses "like" or "as"), we nonetheless see immediately that there is something nonliteral about it: "the enemies of the LORD . . . vanish—like smoke" (Ps. 37:20).

With the figures of speech covered below, we take an even bigger step into the nonliteral. At the end of this chapter I will theorize about why poets resort to the nonliteral and the effects that result when they do. But first we need to abandon ourselves to the poets' project of making unreality at the surface level of their poems.

Hyperbole

I have decided to start with the most nonliteral figure of speech. It is called *hyperbole,* which can be defined as conscious exaggeration for the sake of effect. Often (but not always) the effect aimed at is the expression of strong feeling. I think of hyperbole as being not literally or factually true but emotionally true. By emotionally true I mean an accurate portrayal of (or the truth about) the poet's feelings. By means of hyperbole, we understand how strongly the poet feels about something.

Before I provide examples of hyperbole and explore how to interpret the examples, I want to say emphatically that the writers of the Bible did not share a common evangelical skittishness about hyperbole. They resorted to it frequently. If there is one biblical author with whom we particularly associate hyperbole, it is Jesus. Elton Trueblood, in his small classic titled *The Humor of Christ,*[3] said that one of Jesus' most characteristic rhetorical devices was "his use of deliberate exaggeration," which Trueblood called "the giantesque." In statements like the one about a camel going through the eye of a needle, Jesus used the technique of "our conventional Texas story, which no one believes literally, but which everyone remembers." Here are five specimens of hyperbole in the Bible:

- "The cities are great and fortified up to heaven" (Deut. 1:28).
- "By my God I can leap over a wall" (Ps. 18:29).
- "A thousand may fall at your side, ten thousand at your right hand, but it will not come near you" (Ps. 91:7).
- "You are all together beautiful, my love; there is no flaw in you" (Song of Solomon 4:7).
- "Now there are also many other things that Jesus did. Were every one of them to be written, I suppose that the world itself could not contain the books that would be written" (John 21:25).

Why do poets and others use hyperbole? For at least three reasons. First, we ourselves use hyperbole to express strong feeling. Second, hyperbole is an effective way to express strong conviction about something. Finally, hyperbole compels attention. In regard to this latter point, Elton Trueblood correctly says regarding Jesus,

---

3   Elton Trueblood, *The Humor of Christ* (New York: Harper and Row, 1964). All quotations are from pages 47–48.

"By making the statement in such an exaggerated form . . . Christ made sure that it was memorable, whereas a prosy, qualified statement would certainly have been forgotten."

Personification

Personification consists of treating something nonhuman as though it were a person. At the simplest level, this takes the form of giving human attributes, emotions, or physical features to a nonhuman phenomenon. The range of things that are personified in the Bible is huge. The following list names some categories, accompanied by just one example when actually there are many:

- Cities: "God is in the midst of her [Jerusalem]; she shall not be moved" (Ps. 46:5).
- Body parts: "their tongue struts through the earth" (Ps. 73:9).
- Spiritual entities: "sin is crouching at the door" (Gen. 4:7).
- Abstractions: "righteousness and peace kiss each other" (Ps 85:10).
- Emotions: "weeping may tarry for the night" [weeping as overnight house guest] (Ps. 30:5).
- Forces of nature [the largest category]: "the meadows clothe themselves with flocks" (Ps. 65:13).

This is a representative rather than exhaustive list. There is no limit to what a poet might personify.

The readiness with which poets personify a subject teases us into inquiring why they do so. Alternatively (or simultaneously), what are the effects of personification? We can say most immediately that personification makes a subject concrete, and this is what poets do best. We should recall the principle of the primacy of the image in poetry. To personify something makes it a person in our imagination.

A category under this umbrella occurs when a group or a diffuse phenomenon suddenly becomes concentrated and intensified by being treated as a single person. For example, the broad category of epidemic illness becomes much more personal and terrifying when it is pictured as a solitary and malicious stalker: "the pestilence that stalks in darkness" (Ps. 91:6). Blood at a murder scene is shocking in itself, but the generalized picture of a spot of blood becomes even more shocking when it is personified as a voice "crying . . . from the ground" (Gen. 4:10).

Finally, to portray any subject in human terms is to assert a bond between that object and people. If no bond existed, the poet would not assert the kinship. When a force of nature is personified, this kinship can be warm and comforting. Contrariwise, many of the things that biblical poets personify are even more terrifying than they would otherwise be, and the intensity exists because of the phenomenon is treated like a person.

What strategies does personification require of a reader? The first thing we need to do is *identify that personification exists* in a passage. Second, we can be responsive to the vividness that personification confers on an object. We also need to analyze how the effects noted above are at work in a given instance of personification. And we need to allow the point to register with us (yet again) that poetry and figurative language are inherently fictional and fantastic rather than factual. Poets are always playing the game of make-believe, imagining something that is literally nonexistent or untrue. As readers we need to follow the poets in allowing our imagination to soar beyond the literal.

Apostrophe

The figure of speech known as *apostrophe* is a bit complex, and handbooks of literary terms do not all agree on what I am about to assert. All of the definitions agree that when we apostrophize (the verb form of apostrophe) an object or person, we address that subject directly. The stance is one of direct address. Furthermore, there is an inherent fiction about the situation because for one reason or another the object of the address cannot hear and respond (even though the speaker pretends that hearing and responding are possible).

At this point definitions begin to show just a little variation. Some definitions add as a requirement that the object of address be absent and not in the presence of the speaker. An example is David's apostrophe for his dead son Absalom: "O my son Absalom, my son, my son Absalom! Would I had died instead of you"(2 Sam. 18:33). But if I were to address the clock on my wall or the scene that I see outside my window, I believe that it would be an example of apostrophe. Psalm 148 is a string of apostrophes, and some of the phenomena that are addressed might well be within sight of the poet: "Praise him, sun and moon" (v. 3). The one constant is not that the objects that are apostrophized are absent but rather that they cannot really hear and respond. There is an element of fantasy in the situation.

Another common assumption that is not completely accurate is that apostrophe is always combined with personification. Often it *is* combined with personification, as in Paul's famous taunt of death: "O death, where is your victory?" (1 Cor. 15:55). But there is often no *overt* personification involved in apostrophe (except for the pretense that the object of address can hear). For example, in the Song of Solomon the woman apostrophizes the daughters of Jerusalem, who are flesh and blood people, not personifications: "I adjure you, O daughters of Jerusalem, . . . that you not stir up or awaken love until it pleases" (1:5).

What are the principles that govern this figure of speech? The first is that apostrophe belongs to the realm of fantasy and poetic license: an absent person or personified phenomenon cannot literally listen and respond to a speaker. Second, apostrophe is a standard way of expressing strong feeling. When poets or orators apostrophize someone or something, we can rest assured that they feel strongly about the subject under discussion. Often, in fact, apostrophes *create* a sense of excitement in a reader. Third, the range of things that are apostrophized in the Bible is immense. From the Psalms come these specimens: "be warned, O rulers of the earth" (2:10); "depart from me, all you workers of evil" (6:8); "lift up your heads, O gates" (24:7); "love the LORD, all you his saints" (31:23); "glorious things of you are spoken, O city of God" (87:3).

What rules should govern our assimilation of the apostrophes of the Bible? Once again we need to begin by identifying an apostrophe when we read it. We should further identify whether the address is to something absent or present, and whether it incorporates personification. Since apostrophe is a virtual signal that the poet is feeling strong emotion, we need to allow that situation to register with us. We might think of an apostrophe as an emotional signal. Finally, we need to relish apostrophe as part of the poet's love of make-believe. In real life we would be worried if we overheard someone addressing a tree; in poetry we relish it as a holiday from literal reality.

Paradox

Paradox is another of the "fun" figures of speech that allows us to take a holiday from the literal. With paradox, too, handbooks and dictionaries of literary terms do not wholly agree; what follows are the rules that will prevail in this guided study to biblical poetry. What all the definitions agree on is that a paradox states a contradiction. Matthew 16:25 provides an example: "whoever would save his life will lose it, but whoever loses his life for my sake will find it."

The viewpoint of this book is that a paradox needs to be defined as *an apparent contradiction* only. It turns out to be not a contradiction after all. So the right definition of paradox is that it is an apparent contradiction that, upon analysis, is seen to express a truth. Here are four examples of paradox in the Bible:

- "The mercy of the wicked is cruel" (Prov. 12:10).
- "Faithful are the wounds of a friend; / profuse are the kisses of an enemy" (Prov. 27:6; paraphrased, "The wounds of a friend are better than the kisses of an enemy").
- "The last will be first, and the first last" (Matt. 20:16).
- "When I am weak, then I am strong" (2 Cor. 12:10).

The important interpretive point regarding paradox is that the seeming contradiction *needs to be resolved* in order for the truth of the statement to emerge.

We need to observe at once that pure examples of paradox such as the examples cited above are relatively rare in the Bible. But with a flexible and broadened application of the principle explained above, paradox is a major figurative device in the Bible. The looser definition is a statement that uses heightened contrasts in terse construction so that the effect is like that of a pure paradox, namely, that it initially strikes us as implausible. Only with analysis (as in pure paradox) do we see the truth of the statement. Here are four examples:

- "For the foolishness of God is wiser than men, and the weakness of God is stronger than men" (1 Cor. 1:25).
- "We are . . . persecuted, but not forsaken; struck down, but not destroyed" (2 Cor. 4:8-9).
- "He came to his own, and his own people did not receive him" (John 1:11).
- "The meek shall inherit the land" (Ps. 37:11).

Our initial response is to wonder, How can that be? Then we analyze the situation and find a way to explain it. When we thus resolve the heightened contrast (bordering on contradiction), we have resolved the paradox.

With the Psalms, an even broader definition is possible, especially in regard to the lament psalms. The lament psalms contain five main parts, and they always include an element of recantation. In effect, the poet begins by asserting that his situation is hopeless, and suddenly, without transition, he asserts that the situation isn't hopeless after all but that God will act (or has already acted) to save the speaker (or the righteous for whom he speaks). This situation lends itself to treatment as a paradox: how can a hopeless situation not be hopeless after all?

Paradox is based on the premise of jolting readers or listeners out of complacency and activating them to make sense of what seems to be a nonsense statement. A paradox is a riddle—something that does not make immediate sense and that therefore teases us into discovering what it means. Many scholarly and Internet sources erroneously define oxymoron as though it were paradox. An oxymoron is a genuine contradiction that embraces both halves of a contradiction and that cannot be "explained away" as we do with paradox. If we can resolve the seeming contradiction, it is a paradox, not an oxymoron.

Part of the appeal of paradox is that it overcomes the cliché effect of acknowledged truths. When the familiar truth is expressed in the form of a riddle, we are inclined to take note. Along with that, there is something subversive about a paradox. It undermines conventional ways of thinking and defies the "wisdom" of the world.

What methodology does paradox require of a reader? We need to identify the seeming contradiction and then bring our powers of analysis and reasoning to bear and explain how the apparent contradiction can be resolved and therefore express truth.

Metonymy, Synecdoche, and Merism

Now we are getting to the "fine print" and the difficult to pronounce! There is no claim made here that these are major poetic forms in the Bible. But when we come upon them, we need to know what to do with them, so it is entirely appropriate to take stock of them.

Metonymy consists of naming something by means of something else to with which it is closely associated. Some handbooks call it "substitute naming" because a word is substituted in place of the actual thing being discussed. For example, when Jesus told Zacchaeus that "today salvation has come to this house" (Luke 19:9), he meant that salvation had come to the person who lived in the house. To "drink the cup" of communion (1 Cor. 11:26) means to drink the wine or juice that is in the cup. In the proverb that "the lips of the righteous feed many" (Prov. 10:21), the word "lips" means words that are spoken with one's lips. When Nathan tells David that "the sword shall never depart from your house" (2 Sam. 12:10), he uses two metonymies—sword for violence and house for family.

As always with figures of speech, correct handling of metonymy begins by recognizing that something has not been named directly but by means of a substitute. Then it is useful to analyze what effects are gained with the substitution as compared with direct naming. Overall, a poet or speaker might use metonymy for the sake of fresh expression, jolting us out of the indifference that often attends the overly familiar or expected.

Synecdoche consists of using part of something to signify the whole phenomenon. For example, in the petition in the Lord's Prayer "give us this day our daily bread" (Matt. 6:11), bread represents all the things required to sustain physical life. When the psalmist says that "all my bones shall say" (Ps. 35:10), he means that his entire being will speak. When the wisdom teacher says about violent people that "their feet run to evil" (Prov. 1:16), we are to understand that their whole person is quick to do something evil, with the motion of the feet (a part of the body) representing the motion of the whole person.

The rules for interpreting synecdoche are the same as those for metonymy. Statements that use synecdoche seem so natural that on a quick reading we scarcely notice that the statement is something other than a direct statement. Once we identify a statement as using synecdoche, we can get mileage out of analyzing why the poet used the specific part to stand for the whole. What is the effect when, instead of saying that wicked person is full of deceit and oppression, the poet wrote, "His mouth is filled with cursing and deceit and oppression" (Ps. 10:7).

The figure of speech known as *merism* appears regularly in the Bible, and rarely in English and American poetry. It consists of naming two opposites with the intention that we interpret these polar opposites as together encompassing everything between as well as at the poles. We might think of it as the A-to-Z principle—the beginning and end and everything between. Here are five examples from the Psalms:

- Job's recollection of how revered he was when he was prosperous: "the young men saw me and withdrew, / and the aged rose and stood" (Job 29:8; the meaning: everyone held Job in reverence).
- "The sun shall not strike you by day, / nor the moon by night" (Ps. 121:6; the meaning: God will protect you at all times).
- "You know when I sit down and when I rise up" (Ps. 139:2; the meaning: you know everything about my all that I do);
- "Awake, O north wind, / and come, O south wind" (Song 4:16; the implied meaning: all wind, from every direction).

- "Many will come from east and west" (Matt. 8:11; the meaning: from everywhere).

It is extremely important to pick up on merism when it exists; if we do not, we will misinterpret the statement. Our immediate response to a merism is to look at the opposites and think in terms of division and dichotomy. That is exactly wrong with merism, where the meaning is not division but the opposite of that—wholeness and completeness.

Symbol and Anthropomorphism

The *symbol* (or *symbolism*) is an extremely important figure of speech, but it is a bit elusive. I might have housed it in the chapter on metaphor and simile. Double meaning is at the heart of symbolism. A symbol first of all is what the poet states—a crown, for example. But in symbolism this literal phenomenon also represents or stands for or signifies a second level of meaning. Thus a crown symbolizes a king and kingly power.

To get a handle on how symbolism works and what it requires of us in interpreting it, we can use the reference to the Promised Land of the Old Testament as a land that "flows with milk and honey"(Num. 13:27). We need to start with the literal properties of milk and honey. Milk was a staple in the ancient world (on a par with bread). Honey was valued for its sweetness and ranked as a luxury. So those complementary qualities are part of the symbolic meaning of the reference to a land flowing with milk and honey. But if we look at the places where the paired images of milk and honey occur (over twenty times in the Bible), the symbolism reaches out to include associations of abundance, goodness, and contentment—the "best of the best" principle. The Promised Land did not simply possess the things symbolized by milk and honey—it *flowed* with them.

A symbol operates much as a metaphor does, and it is often a judgment call as to whether we call something a symbol or a metaphor. The farther removed a statement is from the formula that A is like B, the more natural it seems to call it a symbol. For example, in Psalm 42, as the poet living in exile among pagans laments his despair and the oppressiveness of his pagan environment, he says that "your waves have gone over me" (v. 7). Then two verses later he calls God his rock. Are these metaphors? The idea of comparison is so remote in the passage that it seems more helpful to call the torrents and the rock symbols.

What interpretive methods does a symbol require of us? We need to start with the object in its own right—water, for example, or cup. Having assimilated the properties of that thing, we need to ponder what those qualities tell us about the thing symbolized. It is important to take the time to ponder the multiple meanings of a symbol. For example, light and darkness are two of the most many-sided symbols in the Bible, but if we do not take time to unpack their meanings, they become thin—clichés and abstractions instead of evocative symbols.

Does symbolism fall under the rubric of nonliteral? It does, in the same way that metaphor does. A symbol points to something beyond itself (a second level of meaning), and this thing referred to is not literally the same as the symbol. For example, the lamb is a symbol of Christ, but Christ is not literally a lamb.

An additional figure of speech is known as *anthropomorphism.* That is a big word, but we cannot deal with the Bible well without having it in our repertoire of literary terms. Anthropomorphism consists of portraying deity in human terms. There is an incipient symbolism in anthropomorphism, as human qualities are attributed to God even though we know that God is not a human.

One category within the sphere of anthropomorphism consists of ascribing body parts to God, as God is repeatedly said to have a hand and arm and foot. Another category is human actions, such as leading an army, engaging in single combat with a nation, and sleeping and needing to be aroused ("the sleeping God" motif). Elsewhere God is pictured as changing his mind, thinking things through the way a person does, or going on a fact-finding mission to see what is happening in a given locale on earth (e.g., Gen. 18:17–21 for examples of the latter two categories).

Anthropomorphism is a figure of speech and must be understood as nonliteral. In primitive religions, anthropomorphism often signals a belief about what the gods are literally like, but the writers of the Bible make it clear that they know that God is a supernatural and spiritual being. They are not primitives but poets with a metaphoric imagination.

We need to have the word "anthropomorphism" ready at hand when we read the Bible. If we do not, and if we do not realize that the figure is symbolic rather than literal, we will have a problem both in private reading and in teaching the Bible.

Allusion

Allusion is a very important figure of speech, and I have placed it in this chapter because it needed a home. It does not fit under the heading of unreality or fantasy. It expresses its truth directly.

We do not need a complex or fancy or long definition for allusion. An allusion is a reference to past literature or history. It is as simple as that. Here are four examples:

- "The floods stood up in a heap; / the deeps congealed in the heart of the sea" (Exod. 15:8—an allusion to the circumstances of the Red Sea crossing).
- "By the word of the LORD the heavens were made" (Ps. 33:6—an allusion to the creation story of Genesis 1).

- "He made known his ways to Moses, / his acts to the people of Israel" (Ps. 103:7—an allusion to God's giving Moses the law at Sinai).
- "By faith the walls of Jericho fell down after they had been encircled for seven days" (Heb. 11:30—an allusion to the conquest of Jericho when Israel entered the Promised Land).

Obviously an allusion demands a lot from a reader. If we are not familiar with the work of literature or historical event to which a poet or author alludes, we miss the meaning of a passage completely. The more we know about the thing to which the poet alludes, the more complete will be our understanding of the poet's intended meaning.

We should note in passing that an allusion occurs when an author consciously refers to a specific past work of literature or event from history. Allusion should not be treated as synonymous with a mere reference to something. In Psalm 133, the poet compares unity among believers to (1) the oil that ran down the entire head and garment of Aaron in tabernacle worship and (2) the dew that falls on Mount Hermon. The first of these is an allusion, and the second is a reference but not an allusion.

How does allusion actually function? It is a means of achieving tremendous compression of meaning, and often multiplicity of meaning. Simply by naming the previous literary passage or historical event, the poet unleashes a whole set of meanings associated with this previous thing. When we read in Psalm 136:10 that God "struck down the firstborn of Egypt," the poet taps into the entire story of the tenth plague. Without the allusion, the poem praising God would be thinner in its meanings.

LEARNING BY DOING

The foregoing inventory of leading figures of speech is a check-list of terms that it is good to have at our disposal. Even when we cannot think of the technical term, our familiarity with the terms makes it more likely that we will recognize a figure of speech and know how to interpret it and extract its meanings. The following passages do not incorporate all of the possible figures of speech, but they provide a good sampling. It is important not to rush the exercise. This is your chance to apply the theory and methodology that have been provided above. Verse by verse, image by image, experience the figure of speech on the first level, and then perform the further interpretive actions that have been described above. For purposes of review, also analyze the figures of speech covered in the preceding two chapters (imagery, metaphor, and simile).

PSALM 114

[1] When Israel went out from Egypt,
> the house of Jacob from a people of strange
> language,
[2] Judah became his sanctuary,
> Israel his dominion.
[3] The sea looked and fled;
> Jordan turned back.
[4] The mountains skipped like rams,
> the hills like lambs.
[5] What ails you, O sea, that you flee?
> O Jordan, that you turn back?
[6] O mountains, that you skip like rams?
> O hills, like lambs?

[7] Tremble, O earth, at the presence of the LORD,
   at the presence of the God of Jacob,
[8] who turns the rock into a pool of water,
   the flint into a spring of water.

PSALM 46

[1] God is our refuge and strength,
   a very present help in trouble.
[2] Therefore we will not fear though the earth gives way,
   though the mountains be moved into the
   heart of the sea,
[3] though its waters roar and foam,
   though the mountains tremble at its swelling.
[4] There is a river whose streams make glad the city of God,
   the holy habitation of the Most High.
[5] God is in the midst of her; she shall not be moved;
   God will help her when morning dawns.
[6] The nations rage, the kingdoms totter;
   he utters his voice, the earth melts.
[7] The LORD of hosts is with us;
   the God of Jacob is our fortress.
[8] Come, behold the works of the LORD,
   how he has brought desolations on the earth.
[9] He makes wars cease to the end of the earth;
   he breaks the bow and shatters the spear;
   he burns the chariots with fire.
[10] "Be still, and know that I am God.
   I will be exalted among the nations,
   I will be exalted in the earth!"
[11] The LORD of hosts is with us;
   the God of Jacob is our fortress.

PSALM 97

[1] The LORD reigns, let the earth rejoice;
      let the many coastlands be glad!
[2] Clouds and thick darkness are all around him;
      righteousness and justice are the foundation
      of his throne.
[3] Fire goes before him
      and burns up his adversaries all around.
[4] His lightnings light up the world;
      the earth sees and trembles.
[5] The mountains melt like wax before the LORD,
      before the LORD of all the earth.
[6] The heavens proclaim his righteousness,
      and all the peoples see his glory.
[7] All worshipers of images are put to shame,
      who make their boast in worthless idols;
      worship him, all you gods!
[8] Zion hears and is glad,
      and the daughters of Judah rejoice,
      because of your judgments, O LORD.
[9] For you, O LORD, are most high over all the earth;
      you are exalted far above all gods.
[10] O you who love the LORD, hate evil!
      He preserves the lives of his saints;
      he delivers them from the hand of the wicked.
[11] Light is sown for the righteous,
      and joy for the upright in heart.
[12] Rejoice in the LORD, O you righteous,
      and give thanks to his holy name!

Final Thoughts on Biblical Poetry

This chapter has introduced a menu of technical terms. The terms are not difficult, and there is no reason not to familiarize ourselves with them. There are only three difficult terms. One is anthropomorphism, which is so important (and appears so often) that we have no choice but to memorize it. Metonymy and synecdoche are also difficult. Knowing the words is optional; what is important is that we recognize when a closely related term is substituted for the actual subject under consideration (metonymy) and when a part is used to stand for the whole (synecdoche).

Beyond that, the terms for figures of speech are entirely manageable. Even though knowing the terms is very useful, it is nonetheless important that the point register with us that merely naming a figure of speech accurately is of very limited usefulness when we are reading or teaching biblical poetry. In fact, it is almost useless by itself. What matters is that we unpack the meanings that are embodied in a figure of speech. Identifying a figure of speech accurately is merely a useful aid to exploring the meanings that the poet expresses by means of it.

Why do poets speak in figures of speech? The first answer is that they do so in the interests of meaning. In terms appropriate to a given figure of speech, poets speak in the manner that most accurately communicates their message. This is simply a vote of confidence that we need to give to poets.

Additionally, figurative language achieves freshness of expression. It overcomes the cliché effect of straightforward expository prose. Poetry possesses arresting strangeness. We need to relish it for that quality.

Summary

Poets speak a language all their own. We need to master the language that they speak. To our surprise, poets prefer the nonliteral to the literal—not absolutely, but most of the time. The fact that a third of the Bible is poetic in form should lead us to conclude that poetry is important to us. We can learn to understand and enjoy it.

Artistic Beauty

The Parallelism of Biblical Poetry

An essential feature of poetry is that a poem is embodied in a verse form. In most languages, the verse form consists of meter and rhythm, line length, and a rhyme scheme at the ends of the lines. The verse form of biblical poetry does not use rhyme but instead consists of thought couplets. The two lines are artfully constructed to form a unit together. Because something in the second line answers to something in the first line, this verse form is known as *parallelism*.

The purpose of this chapter is to explain the types of parallelism in biblical poetry. This is useful information, and there are occasions when analyzing the verse form of a poem or passage yields important results. Nonetheless, it is important to realize right from the start that the verse form of parallelism is not the aspect of poetry that embodies the meanings. The imagery and figures of speech embody the message. Parallelism is only the vehicle in which the figurative language is packaged. Because biblical scholars generally do not know how to handle poetic language, they often attempt to get an analytic mileage out of parallelism that it does not possess.

The Types of Biblical Parallelism

I will begin my exploration with an anatomy of types of biblical parallelism. It will not be useful to talk about the effects of parallelism if we do not have the phenomenon itself clearly in our minds. I will theorize about the effects of parallelism in the subsequent unit of the chapter.

Before we note the specific types of biblical parallelism, we should pause to understand the concept of parallelism as a universal (what all types of parallelism share in common). In any sphere of life, parallelism exists only with two or more units. In biblical poetry, these units are consecutive lines of poetry. In biblical parallelism, all or part of the second line matches or is parallel to something in the first line. Additionally, the two lines usually use the same grammatical structure and the same syntax (sentence elements).

To keep the subject manageable, I will be considering only two-line examples of parallelism. Nonetheless, it is not uncommon for biblical parallelism to entail three lines or four lines or even more.

Synonymous Parallelism

In *synonymous parallelism,* the second line restates all or part of the first line in different words or images. The second line also uses the same grammatical form and sentence structure as the first line (on the understanding that often only *part* of the first line is paralleled by something in the second line). An example of complete parallelism is the following:

> The LORD of hosts is with us;
>> the God of Jacob is our fortress. (Ps. 46:7)

The three main units of line 1 (subject, verb, predicate) are matched by corresponding units in the second line, as follows: The LORD of hosts / the God of Jacob; is / is; with us / our refuge.

In the following example, only part of the second line matches something in the first:

> The LORD works righteousness
> > and justice for all who are oppressed. (Ps. 103:6)

The subject and verb ("the LORD works") is omitted from the second line. The entire construction "justice for all who are oppressed" is understood to be parallel to the word "righteousness" in the first line. Grammatically these two parallel units are direct objects of the verb "works."

Antithetic Parallelism

In antithetic parallelism, the second line states the truth of the first line in a contrasting way. In the most overt situations, the poet starts the second line with the coordinating word "but":

> The light of the righteous rejoices,
> > but the lamp of the wicked will be put out. (Prov. 13:9)

The "light" and "lamp" are parallel in both grammatical form and content, while the prepositional phrases "of the righteous" and "of the wicked" are contrasted at the level of content (even though grammatically they are the same), and the concluding verbs ("rejoices" and "will be put out") are grammatically parallel but opposite in meaning.

When the word "but" does not appear at the beginning of the second line, the contrast is more subtle, and we may need to ponder the passage before we see the contrast. Here is an example:

> Faithful are the wounds of a friend;
> > profuse are the kisses of an enemy. (Prov. 27:6)

We should start by noting the strict grammatical and syntactic parallels: "faithful" and "profuse"; "are" and "are"; "the wounds" and "the kisses"; "of a friend" and "of an enemy." However, a whole network of contrasts is at work in the statement—wounds (constructive criticism) versus kisses (flattery), friend versus enemy, and constructive intention to build up (*faithful*) versus deception (*profuse kisses*) that conceals an intention to destroy.

Synthetic Parallelism

Synthetic parallelism should be thought of *growing parallelism* or *expanding parallelism*. The second line completes something that was introduced in the first line. Here is an example:

> These all look to you,
>> to give them their food in due season. (Ps. 104:27)

The second line completes the first, but strictly speaking there is nothing in the second line that parallels anything in the first line. The second line simply completes the thought that began in the first line.

Why then is it called parallelism? Because it shares important qualities with other forms of parallelism. The two lines belong together and form a thought couplet. As with other forms of parallelism, when we read or hear the first line, we wait "for the second foot to fall" (as the familiar saying has it). Synthetic parallelism sets up a rhythm of contemplation consisting of two lines, as the other forms of parallelism do.

Climactic Parallelism

The tip-off for climactic parallelism is that the second line repeats part of the first line verbatim and then adds to it. Almost always the first line leaves the thought incomplete—dangling in midair until the second line completes it:

Ascribe to the LORD, O families of the peoples,
>   Ascribe to the LORD glory and strength! (Ps. 96:7)

But occasionally the thought is already complete at the end of the first line, and the repetition of a phrase or clause in the second line is simply a pleasing artistic effect and also a way of highlighting something:

In you our fathers trusted;
>   they trusted, and you delivered them. (Ps. 22:4)

The repetition of the verb "trusted" focuses our attention on it and enhances the meaning beyond what would have been achieved if the poet had simply gone on with "and you delivered them."

The Effects of Parallelism

Although I have said that the meaning of biblical poetry resides in the imagery and figurative language, that does not make parallelism unimportant. As I answer the question of how parallelism affects and enriches our experience of biblical poetry, it will be obvious that the verse form of parallelism is important.

First, parallelism is an important part of the artistry and beauty of biblical poetry. C. S. Lewis has gone so far as to claim that parallelism incarnates the very essence of artistry. Parallelism, writes Lewis, "is a very pure example of what all . . . art involves." The principle of art is "the same in the other." Lewis goes on to illustrate this as follows: "In a building there may be a wing on one side and a wing on the other, but both of the same shape."[4]

Second, parallelism is what scholars call a *mnemonic device*— an aid to memorizing and remembering. In Lewis's words, paral-

---

4   C. S. Lewis, *Reflections on the Psalms* (New York: Harcourt, Brace, & World, 1958), 3–4.

lelism makes a statement "almost impossible to forget."[5] This is the utilitarian side of parallelism, to match the artistic side.

Additionally, parallelism is a meditative form. It resists rapid movement away from a statement and has within it a retarding element. The poet allows himself plenty of time before moving on, and the result is that as readers we, too, ponder a statement and stick with it for a "repeat performance." Someone has said that the effect of parallelism is like turning a prism in the light, and also like squeezing all possible nuances out of a statement.

LEARNING BY DOING

Any poetic passage in the Bible can be used to analyze how parallelism works. Psalm 97 is a good test case. The point of printing the psalm here is to allow you to work your way through a specimen poem from the Bible and analyze how parallelism works. The benefits of the exercise depend on your not rushing it. For each verse, identify the type of parallelism and give some thought to how the presence of parallelism contributes to your experience of the poem.

> [1] The LORD reigns, let the earth rejoice;
>> let the many coastlands be glad!
> [2] Clouds and thick darkness are all around him;
>> righteousness and justice are the foundation
>> of his throne.
> [3] Fire goes before him
>> and burns up his adversaries all around.
> [4] His lightnings light up the world;
>> the earth sees and trembles.

5   Ibid., 5

[5]The mountains melt like wax before the LORD,
　　before the LORD of all the earth.
[6]The heavens proclaim his righteousness,
　　and all the peoples see his glory.
[7]All worshipers of images are put to shame,
　　who make their boast in worthless idols;
　　worship him, all you gods!
[8]Zion hears and is glad,
　　and the daughters of Judah rejoice,
　　because of your judgments, O LORD.
[9]For you, O LORD, are most high over all the earth;
　　you are exalted far above all gods.
[10]O you who love the LORD, hate evil!
　　He preserves the lives of his saints;
　　he delivers them from the hand of the wicked.
[11]Light is sown for the righteous,
　　and joy for the upright in heart.
[12]Rejoice in the LORD, O you righteous,
　　and give thanks to his holy name!

Final Thoughts on Biblical Parallelism

While all scholars agree on what I have said thus far, disagreement exists in regard to the overall principle that underlies parallelism. The simple, straightforward theory is as follows, and I have taken the formulation by C. S. Lewis as my guide. In the simple view, parallelism is "the practice of saying the same thing twice in different words."[6] By the phrase "the same thing," Lewis of course does not mean that the second statement is identical with the first

---

6　Ibid., 3.

one; he means that second statement "makes no logical addition" and instead "echoes, with variation, the first."[7] Lewis cautions against the practice of straining "to get different meanings out of each half of the verse."[8]

Surely this is the best way to view biblical parallelism. But some scholars like complexity, so further theories of biblical parallelism exist. Two of them express the same viewpoint in slightly different formulas, but both are in agreement that parallelism is progressive rather than repetitive. In one scholar's formula, we should understand the two lines as asserting, "A, and what's more, B." The other formulation is that the second line conveys the sense "how much more so."

We need to tread cautiously here. Of course the second line can be seen as intensifying the first line through the very fact that it repeats something, but if we reverse the two lines, then it is the original first line that is said to assert "how much more so." I leave it to my readers to decide the degree to which they wish to use the two formulas I have cited. I propose that we need to avoid straining to find a progressive element. Reinforcement in the form of repetition is most often what the poet intended.

We do not need to strain to find progression between the two lines in order to relish the combination of recurrence and innovation in parallelism. Usually something is repeated (except in synthetic parallelism), but something is also added to form a combination of old and new. Additionally, even though there is symmetry between the two lines, usually only part of the first line is paralleled in the second line, with the result that there is asymmetry as well as symmetry. Certainly parallelism is not boring or merely repetitive.

---

7   Ibid., 5.
8   Ibid., 3

Summary

Perhaps the most obvious feature of biblical poetry is the verse form of parallelism. The moment we see poetry on a page of the Bible, we know that it is poetry because of the versification. Parallelism is a form of artistic beauty, and additionally it focuses attention on what is said by the interplay of repetition and innovation, the same and something different, the old and new.

PART 2

The Composition
of Biblical Poems

What We Need to Know about Biblical Poems

The subject of this guided study up to now has been *poetry* —the kind of discourse that poetry is. We might think of it as the building blocks out of which a poet constructs a poem. If poetry is a way or speaking and a form of language, *a poem* is a composition made out of this poetic idiom.

What we call a poem is almost always *a lyric poem.*[9] This is not to say that all poems are lyrics. An oracle in the prophetic books is more often than not expressed in poetic form, but it is not a lyric. The book of Proverbs is poetic in form, but the units are not lyrics. Nonetheless, this chapter will cover the genre of lyric poems. All of

---

9   Lyric poetry is a form of poetry that expresses personal emotions or feelings, typically spoken in the first person. The term derives from a form of ancient Greek literature, the lyric, which was defined by its musical accompaniment, usually on a stringed instrument known as a lyre. The term owes its importance in literary theory to the division developed by Aristotle between three broad categories of poetry: lyrical, dramatic, and epic.

the Psalms and all of the poems in the Song of Solomon are lyrics, as is the Song of Moses (Exod. 15), the Song of Deborah (Judg. 5), and the Christ hymns of the New Testament. I will call these lyrics "poems" because it is a less threatening term. My readers need to keep in mind, however, that I am describing "*lyric* poems" in this chapter, and that this includes the entire book of Psalms.

The Content of a Poem

We can tell a poem partly by its content. That content generally falls into two categories. One path open to a poet is to share a sequence of thoughts with readers. Such a poem is not simply a collection of ideas but a person captured in the process of thinking about an issue or experience. We can accurately speak of the resulting poem as a meditative poem or a reflective poem. Thoughts and the process of thinking them through take center stage. Psalm 23 is a reflective poem in which the poet contemplates the sufficiency of God's providence.

The other option is to share feelings or emotions. We can speak of the resulting poem as being an affective or emotional lyric poem. The primary focus is the sequence of feelings that the speaker experiences and shares with us as the poem unfolds. The primary business that such a poem transacts is not intellectual but emotional—a poem of the heart rather than a poem of the head. Virtually all of the individual poems that make the anthology of love poems known as the Song of Solomon are affective poems. Often we can think of affective poems as *mood pieces* that exist to evoke a mood.

General Traits of Poems

The first trait of a lyric poem is *brevity*. Poems capture a feeling at the greatest point of intensity or a thought process at a moment of heightened insight. Intensity and concentration are hallmarks of poems. One cannot prolong a process of thinking or a feeling indefinitely. Lyric poets do not *want* to prolong them. They want the concentrated effect.

The brevity of poems means that they are *self-contained*. They are not chapters in a story. The psalms are "one off" performances. Even the Song of Solomon meets this criterion: all the poems are part of a single romance and marriage between Solomon and his bride, and together they make up an anthology of love poems, but the poems themselves are not chapters in an ongoing story. The book of Psalms is a poetry anthology made up of individual poems.

Another quality that stems from the concentrated brevity of poems is that they rarely intend to be a complete or a thoroughly-thought-out position on a subject. They express a moment of insight or heightened feeling, not a reasoned and complete position. Statements such as "in all that he does, he prospers" (Ps. 1:3) or "no evil shall be allowed to befall you" (Ps. 91:10) express a momentary thought or feeling in a certain optimistic context within the respective poems where they appear, not an absolute rule for all of life.

Poems are also *personal and subjective*. The poet usually speaks in the first-person, "I," format. When the poet has an unusually strong sense of speaking for a group (as in numerous psalms), he uses the first-person plural format ("we," "our"). In view of this personal stance, with many lyric poems we feel as though we overhear the speaker. Often the poet or speaker in effect turns his back on us as he addresses God, nature, himself, enemies, or fellow believers—but rarely us.

Another feature of lyric poems is that they often represent the poet's *response to a stimulus*. We can think of poems as the voice of response. The typical strategy in a lyric poem is for the poet to begin by alerting us to the stimulus that drives the rest of the poem. The range of such stimuli in biblical poetry is nearly limitless—a crisis, the ravages of evil in the world, injustice, nature, God, a worship experience, enemies, victory, an earthly beloved, and more. The more precisely we identify the thing that moves the poet to thought or feeling, the better will be our understanding of a poem.

Finally, the reflective or affective content of lyric poems results in a certain type of movement or flow. That flow can be called *abrupt and disjointed*. C. S. Lewis advises readers of the Psalms that they must expect "the emotional rather than logical connections [that] are proper to lyric poetry."[10] There are certainly psalms and poems in the Song of Solomon that meet all of the classical criteria of shapely form, but most biblical poems are fluid and disjoined in their organization. The designation from modern literature "stream of consciousness" correctly describes many biblical poems, meaning that they jump around and meander as they follow the flow of the mind as it actually operates in real life.

Discerning the Unity of a Poem

It is very debilitating to our understanding of a poem to treat it as a collection of verses. Poems are carefully designed wholes, possessing elaborate unity. This unity is of multiple types. The purpose of this unit and the one that follows it is to put you in possession of how poems are unified and organized.

The unity of a poem is of two different types—ideational and structural. The literary term for ideational unity is *theme*. It denotes the idea that the poem primarily asserts. It is true that some poems assert multiple themes, but the goal of determining the ideational unity of a poem is to see the poem as a single entity. Even if occasionally formulating a statement of theme represents

---

10   C. S. Lewis, *Reflections on the Psalms* (New York: Harcourt, Brace, & World, 1958), 3.

a choice among two or more good options, it is important to make a choice. Another name that has become common for the theme of a poem is "the big idea" of the poem.

A good way to arrive at a statement of the big idea is to follow a two-part sequence. The first step is to state the *topic* of the poem. Sometimes this is actually the human experience that the poet presents, but with other poems the topic is a concept rather than an experience. Having determined what the poem is about (its topic), we need to decide what the poem says *about* that topic. This is the theme.

We can take Psalm 23 as an illustration. Psalm 23 is about God's providence in the lives of those who follow him. The theme is the sufficiency of God's providence. It reaches to all areas of life. But Psalm 23 embodies an attitude of peace and contentment, so it is advisable to put that into the mix as well. The final statement of the big idea is therefore the contentment that comes from resting in the sufficiency of God's providence.

We have never adequately grasped a poem if we do not, after analysis, formulate the big idea of the poem. Nonetheless, it is important to sound a caution at this point. The big idea of the poem is usually not the best way in which to organize the structure of a poem. A poem is a literary composition, not an essay. To slant our interpretation around an idea rather than something more literary makes the poem seem like an essay.

Again we can take Psalm 23 as an illustration. The idea that the poem asserts is the sufficiency of God's providence. If we were to organize the poem around that idea, we would spin out a series of abstract propositions—God provides peace (the green pastures and still waters), protection (the rod and staff), freedom from fear in the face of life's adversities and death (the valley of deepest darkness), food (the prepared table), and so forth. If we talk about the poem in those terms, the actual texture of the poem disappears from sight and we are dealing with the poem with an intellectual construction that we ourselves have built. More will be said about this in the next unit of the chapter.

Ideational unity is one type of unity in a poem; the other type of unity is structural or organizational unity. In turn, structure also falls into two categories. One is spatial unity—the organization of the whole poem at a single glance. The other type of organization is sequential—how the poem unfolds from beginning to end.

The spatial unity of a poem consists of the element of contrast in the poem. The principle of contrast is the poetic equivalent of plot conflict in a story. Most poems are structured as a single overriding contrast or a system of contrasts (some of them limited to local parts of a poem.). An example of an obvious central contrast is Psalm 1, which is structured around a prolonged contrast between "the two ways." Within that central contrast we find a host of smaller contrasts in local parts of the poem.

But the contrasts of a poem are not always that obvious. Sometimes we need to ponder and analyze the poem before we see the system of contrasts in it. The advantage of knowing that most poems are structured on contrasts is that it prompts us to identify the element of contrast in the poem. Psalm 23 *seems* to be a serene, straightforward picture of a shepherd's provisions for his sheep during the course of a typical day. But the positive picture of daily provision is presented against a backdrop of threats to the sheep. The list of threats is extensive: drought and the scarcity of grass and water that it brings; walking between the sheepfold and places of grazing and watering over a treacherous terrain full of possibilities for mishap; dark valleys that instill fear; predators; poisonous plants; scratches and cuts that require treatment in the sheepfold at the end of the day (the images of anointing and the overflowing cup).

To sum up, we have looked thus far at two types of spatial unity in a poem—the unity that allows us to see the whole poem at once. These two types are ideational unity and a system of contrasts that operates throughout the poem and is not dependent on the sequential unfolding of the poem. But poems also unfold by a series of steps from beginning to end. This is the poem's sequential unity and structure. Sequential structure is such a complex phenomenon that it requires a separate unit in this chapter.

Sequential Structure

The simplest form of sequential structure is the paradigm of a three-part design. This tripartite model is the basic format for nearly all written compositions. It is the format of beginning-middle-end. The resulting composition is coherent, whole, and complete.

The opening movement of a poem advertises that it is an opening—act 1 of a three-part drama. The poet begins by hinting or plainly stating what the poem is about. In keeping with the nature of lyric (the voice of response), we can often look upon this opening situation as *the stimulus* that gives rise to the rest of the poem. This stimulus can be an idea, a feeling, a state of mind, an address to an audience or to God, or a situation.

It is important that we grasp the helpfulness of the poem's opening as a guide to the rest of the poem. It is like a sign over an entrance. We can trust the poet to have chosen the opening lines carefully. Here is a random list of examples:

- "Fret not yourself because of evildoers." (Ps. 37:1)
- "Vindicate me, O God, and defend my cause / against an ungodly people." (Ps. 43:1)
- "Shout for joy to God, all the earth." (Ps. 66:1)
- "Those who trust in the LORD are like Mount Zion, / which cannot be moved, but abides forever." (Ps. 125:1)

All of these openings are pointers that announce the subject and set the tone for what we will find in the rest of the poem.

The conclusion of a poem is as ritualistic as we have just seen the openings to be. Poems do not simply end; they are rounded off with a note of closure, resolution, and finality. The conclusion might be a recapitulation of what has preceded, or it might consist of a conventional prayer or wish. Here are five typical examples:

- "Rejoice in the LORD, O you righteous, / and give thanks to his holy name!" (Ps. 97:12)
- "Praise the LORD!" (Ps. 113:9)
- "Peace be upon Israel!" (Ps. 125:5)
- "The LORD of hosts is with us; / the God of Jacob is our fortress." (Ps. 46:110)
- "Surely goodness and mercy shall follow me / all the days of my life, / and I shall dwell in the house of the LORD forever." (Ps. 23:6)

If we consider the opening and closing of a poem, we see a shapeliness and symmetry that are comparable to a picture that is framed.

What about the middle that exists between the symmetrical opening and closing? This is where the situation starts to get complex.

While there are multiple ways in which a poet can develop the opening theme or statement of stimulus, the most common one is the list or catalog. We should not automatically assume that this will comprise the middle of a poem, but it is common, and additionally it is important that we know how to handle a catalog.

The essential principle is to ascertain the separate units that make up the catalog. We need to put "like with like" and separate units from what is unlike them. The basis of division might be topical or ideational, or a shift in emotion, or changes in imagery.

The units need to be labeled in keeping with what we ascertain to the overall unity of the poem. Here is an example of a catalog in the middle part of Psalm 9:

⁵You have rebuked the nations; you have made the
wicked perish;
>you have blotted out their name forever and
>ever.
⁶The enemy came to an end in everlasting ruins;
>their cities you rooted out;
>the very memory of them has perished.
⁷But the LORD sits enthroned forever;
>he has established his throne for justice,
⁸and he judges the world with righteousness;
>he judges the peoples with uprightness.
⁹The LORD is a stronghold for the oppressed,
>a stronghold in times of trouble.
¹⁰And those who know your name put their trust in you,
>for you, O LORD, have not forsaken those
>who seek you.

This unit comes from a psalm of praise. The unifying theme of the passage is God's praiseworthy acts. The poet develops this theme with a catalog of God's acts. Our task is to divide the catalog into its units. They are as follows: verses 5–6 narrate God's defeat of the wicked; verses 7–8 follow that up with a celebration of God's justice; and verses 9–10 asserts that God can be trusted to protect those who put their trust in him.

There are numerous other ways to develop the opening statement of situation or theme, and these will receive fuller explanation below and in the next chapter. Before we leave the subject now, however, I need to sound a caution (or even state a warning). It is as follows: the tidy outlines that we often find in study

Bibles and commentaries make many psalms look more unified and orderly than they really are. We need to resist such simplifications. Our loyalty must be to what we actually we find in the text before us. Many psalms are, indeed, beautifully organized and meet all the requirements of classical symmetry and form. But many of the psalms are very miscellaneous and disorganized. We need to acknowledge that and not apologize for it or try to compensate for it.

On the other hand, we do not want to capitulate to another common fallacy—that the psalms are a collection of individual verses, to be treated as self-contained small units. Modern poetry has bequeathed to us the terminology and technique known as stream of consciousness. It consists of organizing a poem the way a person thinks and feels in many situations of life—the stream of what goes on in a person's consciousness. This is not the same as a collection of self-contained ideas or feelings; it is *a stream* of ideas and feelings. The point of unity is that the passage before us is a process of thinking and feeling experienced and recorded by the poet. Literary scholars sometimes call this *psychological structure* to denote that the passage is unified by being the thought process that is going on inside the mind of the poet. Here is an example of stream of consciousness structure in Psalm 116:

> ³ The snares of death encompassed me;
>> the pangs of Sheol laid hold on me;
>> I suffered distress and anguish.
> ⁴ Then I called on the name of the LORD:
>> "O LORD, I pray, deliver my soul!"
> ⁵ Gracious is the LORD, and righteous;
>> our God is merciful.
> ⁶ The LORD preserves the simple;
>> when I was brought low, he saved me.

[7]Return, O my soul, to your rest;

for the LORD has dealt bountifully with you.

[8]For you have delivered my soul from death,

my eyes from tears,

my feet from stumbling;

[9]I will walk before the LORD

in the land of the living.

[10]I believed, even when I spoke:

"I am greatly afflicted";

[11]I said in my alarm,

"All mankind are liars."

[12]What shall I render to the LORD

for all his benefits to me?

[13]I will lift up the cup of salvation

and call on the name of the LORD,

[14]I will pay my vows to the LORD

in the presence of all his people.

[15]Precious in the sight of the LORD

is the death of his saints.

If we look at the lines closely, they are all over the place. The thoughts jump abruptly from one thought to something quite different. With ingenuity, we can make the passage look tidy, and this is what published outlines specialize in. The point is not that there is no value in finding more unity than appears at first to be present. The point is that we do not *need* to resort to ingenuity; a poem that presents us with the thought process going on inside the poet's mind can be a unified statement in our own experience of a poem.

To sum up the territory covered in this unit, we have looked at the sequential structure of a poem under the rubric of a three-part structure—introduction, development, and conclusion. There are many ways in which a poet can fill in the middle part of a poem;

we have looked at the catalog technique and a principle of organization known as stream of consciousness. The most important principle of poetic organization by far is something in addition to these, and it requires a section by itself.

Theme and Variation

It is from the field of music that we get the concept of theme and variation. This paradigm is how many pieces of music are structured. It so happens that the same model can be applied to poems.

The first thing we need to do is define the word "theme," and immediately a complexity arises. We have already used the word "theme" to denote the idea that governs a poem. When we speak of theme and variation, theme is likely to denote something more literary than an idea. Here it means literary motif or unifying core (usually not an idea). We need to have an example before us, and Psalm 23 can again come to our aid (it is the world's greatest poem). The unifying theme in the second sense is the acts of provision that a shepherd performs for his sheep in a typical day (the "ideal day" of the pastoral tradition). This is what the poem actually presents, whereas the big idea of God's providence in the lives of people is a conceptual substitute for the shepherd references in the poem.

What, then, are the variations on the theme? They are the individual units that develop the unifying motif of the poem. They need to be phrased in terms that relate to the unifying theme and keep it in view. For Psalm 23, the variations (the specific acts of provision) include the following: noontime rest in an oasis-type place (lying down in green pastures); leading the sheep in safe paths during the course of the day; protecting sheep from fear in dangerous places on the path; finding strips of grass for grazing (the prepared table); protecting the sheep from predators and poisonous plants (the enemies of v. 5); dealing with scratches or cuts and attending to fevered sheep (the anointed head and overflowing cup); and safety overnight in the sheepfold (the metaphoric "house" at the end of the poem).

The scheme of theme and variation imposes a double obligation on us. The first is to formulate a statement of the unifying motif of the poem. It needs to be comprehensive enough to cover the entire poem. It needs to speak directly to the literal surface of the poem—what the poet actually puts before us, not a conceptual framework of our own devising.

Second, the concept of variations on the theme requires that we show how a given unit relates directly to the announced theme. In other words, the idea of theme and variation is a specific manifestation of something that has always been regarded as important in many areas of life—the whole-part relationship.

It is impossible to overstate the usefulness of the methodology of theme and variation. It is our best ally in showing the sequential structure of a poem. It actually generates analytic insights into a poem in the sense that we see more and more in the poem when we are forced to label a given unit in keeping with the announced unifying motif. The test is practical— just start applying the framework and see what it yields.

Psalm 73 as an Illustration

The foregoing sections have explained what we need to know and apply in regard to compositions known as poems. It is time to bring this diffuse material into focus, and Psalm 73 is an ideal text with which to do it.

> [1] Truly God is good to the upright
> (RSV and others; ESV, Israel],
> > to those who are pure in heart.
> [2] But as for me, my feet had almost stumbled,
> > my steps had nearly slipped.

³For I was envious of the arrogant
      when I saw the prosperity of the wicked.
⁴For they have no pangs until death;
      their bodies are fat and sleek.
⁵They are not in trouble as others are;
      they are not stricken like the rest of mankind.
⁶Therefore pride is their necklace;
      violence covers them as a garment.
⁷Their eyes swell out through fatness;
      their hearts overflow with follies.
⁸They scoff and speak with malice;
      loftily they threaten oppression.
⁹They set their mouths against the heavens,
      and their tongue struts through the earth.
¹⁰Therefore his people turn back to them,
      and find no fault in them.
¹¹And they say, "How can God know?
      Is there knowledge in the Most High?"
¹²Behold, these are the wicked;
      always at ease, they increase in riches.
¹³All in vain have I kept my heart clean
      and washed my hands in innocence.
¹⁴For all the day long I have been stricken
      and rebuked every morning.
¹⁵If I had said, "I will speak thus,"
      I would have betrayed the generation of your
      children.
¹⁶But when I thought how to understand this,
      it seemed to me a wearisome task,
¹⁷until I went into the sanctuary of God;
      then I discerned their end.

[18] Truly you set them in slippery places;
>> you make them fall to ruin.
[19] How they are destroyed in a moment,
>> swept away utterly by terrors!
[20] Like a dream when one awakes,
>>> O LORD, when you rouse yourself, you
>>> despise them as phantoms.
[21] When my soul was embittered,
>> when I was pricked in heart,
[22] I was brutish and ignorant;
>> I was like a beast toward you.
[23] Nevertheless, I am continually with you;
>> you hold my right hand.
[24] You guide me with your counsel,
>> and afterward you will receive me to glory.
[25] Whom have I in heaven but you?
>> And there is nothing on earth that I desire
>> besides you.
[26] My flesh and my heart may fail,
>> but God is the strength of my heart and my
>> portion forever.
[27] For behold, those who are far from you shall perish;
>> you put an end to everyone who is unfaithful
>> to you.
[28] But for me it is good to be near God;
>> I have made the LORD God my refuge,
>> that I may tell of all your works.

Application of the various considerations and grids that were presented earlier in this chapter yields the following results:

- *Basic type:* A reflective poem rather than emotional or affective; additionally, the poem has a narrative cast (rare in lyric poetry), in which the poet recounts a series of outer and inward events in their chronological order.

- *Unifying motif* (*theme in the literary rather than ideational sense*): The speaker's crisis of faith. Everything in the poem relates to this crisis—its cause, its detrimental spiritual effects in the speaker's life, its solution, and the speaker's final state of soul (faith regained).

- *Theme in the ideational sense* (*the unifying big idea*): The spiritual and eternal rewards of godliness far outweigh the earthly and temporary rewards of the godless.

- *Three-part format.* First we should isolate verses 1 and 27–28. They provide an envelope structure for the poem by expressing the same sentiment at the beginning and end. This provides a classical sense of symmetry. Between these two bookends, the poet gives us variations on the theme announced early and late, explaining exactly how it is that God is good to the upright and how it is good to be near God.

- *Underlying contrasts*: The problem contrasted to its solution; an almost-fatal crisis of faith contrasted to the speaker's renewal of faith; present, tangible, and earthly matters in the first half versus future, spiritual, and heavenly matters in the second half; the wicked versus the godly; earthly success versus spiritual values; materialism versus godliness; the temporary versus the permanent; error versus truth; doubt versus faith; and apparent reality or illusion versus true and ultimate reality.

- *Variations on the central motif* (*theme in the literary rather than ideational sense*):
  - Preview of the speaker's final state of soul and of his crisis (vv. 1–3).

- o The cause of the speaker's doubt: the prosperity of the wicked (vv. 4–12).
- o The speaker's personal crisis of faith: doubt about whether the godly life is worth the effort (vv. 13–15).
- o The speaker's sudden conquest of his crisis of faith and doubt (vv. 16–17).
- o A second view of the wicked—an explanation of why the speaker changed his mind and how he conquered his doubt (vv. 18–22).
- o A second view of godliness—a spiritual inventory that represents the speaker's renewal of faith and conquest of his crisis of faith (vv. 23–28).

This is one of the greatest poems in the book of Psalms, and much more could be done with the variations on the main theme. However, the foregoing will suffice to illustrate the main concepts covered in this chapter regarding what a poem is and how it does its work.

LEARNING BY DOING

The purpose of this chapter is to cover the distinguishing features of poems, not the poetic language out of which poems are built (the subject of earlier chapters). The goal of the following exercise on Psalm 103 is to apply the categories that have been explained in this chapter, including the following:

- *Content*: Is this a reflective poem in which ideas dominate or an affective poem in which emotions dominate?
- *Unifying motif*: What is the literary motif that unifies the entire poem and to which all the parts relate? Tip: the motif that unifies the poem is asserted right in the poem

in the opening and closing sections with the words "benefits" (v. 2) and "works" (v. 22).

- *Ideational theme*: What is the big idea that the entire poem asserts? Tip: if the poem is about God's acts, what does it say *about* that subject?
- *Contrasts*: What contrasts organize the poem?
- *Three-part structure*: How does the paradigm of a three-part movement manifest itself?
- *Sequential structure*: What are the successive units, and how does each one relate to (or develop) the unifying motif or theme?

[1] Bless the LORD, O my soul,
> and all that is within me,
> bless his holy name!

[2] Bless the LORD, O my soul,
> and forget not all his benefits,

[3] who forgives all your iniquity,
> who heals all your diseases,

[4] who redeems your life from the pit,
> who crowns you with steadfast love and mercy,

[5] who satisfies you with good
> so that your youth is renewed like the eagle's.

[6] The LORD works righteousness
> and justice for all who are oppressed.

[7] He made known his ways to Moses,
> his acts to the people of Israel.

[8] The LORD is merciful and gracious,
> slow to anger and abounding in steadfast love.

[9] He will not always chide,
> nor will he keep his anger forever.

[10] He does not deal with us according to our sins,
       nor repay us according to our iniquities.
[11] For as high as the heavens are above the earth,
       so great is his steadfast love toward those who
       fear him;
[12] as far as the east is from the west,
       so far does he remove our transgressions from us.
[13] As a father shows compassion to his children,
       so the LORD shows compassion to those who
       fear him.
[14] For he knows our frame;
       he remembers that we are dust.
[15] As for man, his days are like grass;
       he flourishes like a flower of the field;
[16] for the wind passes over it, and it is gone,
       and its place knows it no more.
[17] But the steadfast love of the LORD is from everlasting to
  everlasting
       on those who fear him,
       and his righteousness to children's children,
[18] to those who keep his covenant
       and remember to do his commandments.
[19] The LORD has established his throne in the heavens,
       and his kingdom rules over all.
[20] Bless the LORD, O you his angels,
       you mighty ones who do his word,
       obeying the voice of his word!
[21] Bless the LORD, all his hosts,
       his ministers, who do his will!
[22] Bless the LORD, all his works,
       in all places of his dominion.
  Bless the LORD, O my soul!

Final Thoughts on How Poems Work

Previous chapters in this book explored the language that poets use (imagery and figures of speech). This poetic idiom is what actually embodies a poem's meaning. But without the format or packaging of the poem (the material covered in this chapter), a poem's meaning remains largely inaccessible. At best it will be a . collection of tiny individual units.

It is the poem—the composition made up the poetic language—that *enables* the meanings to emerge. Only when we assemble the "container" will the poem take shape for us. This container includes an awareness that (1) the poem is either reflective or emotional in basic content, (2) asserts a big idea, (3) has a spatial structure consisting of one or more underlying contrasts, (4) and possesses a sequential organization. Once we identify these things, the individual poetic elements can take shape in our mind.

All of this conforms to a well-established fact of teaching and comprehension. Educational research has proven that without a unifying framework or superstructure, people do not do a good job of comprehending and remembering a mass of data. The unity and structure of a poem provide such a framework or superstructure.

The material presented earlier in this chapter covers the basics in regard to the sequential structure of a poem (how it unfolds from beginning to end). The primary frameworks for uncovering the progression of a poem are three-part structure (beginning-development-closing) and theme and variation. Some very helpful additional grids are available for people who want that degree of complexity in their analysis of a poem.

One is to be aware that when developing the announced theme of the poem (the middle of the poem), poets have four options at their disposal. Two have been covered above—the catalog or list, and the principle of contrast. The other two options are

(1) repetition (which implies less variation than a catalog possesses) and (2) association. In the second of these, the poet branches out from the initial situation or idea to a related one. In Psalm 19, for example, the poet begins by contemplating God's revelation of himself in nature and then moves to God's revelation of himself in the law.

We can also identify a poem's structure in terms of the type of material that dominates. There are four types of structure based on what material controls the poem:

- *Expository structure*: The poet shares or gives an exposition of either ideas or feelings.
- *Descriptive structure*: The poet describes either a scene or a character.
- *Dramatic structure*: The poet addresses a stated or implied listener or audience.
- *Narrative structure*: The poem narrates a series of events.

It is a matter of personal preference as to whether you wish to apply this gird. I apply this grid to every poem that I analyze and teach.

Summary

A poem is more than simply poetry (images and figures of speech); it is a composition that possesses identifiable traits. Part of the shape or external form of a poem has to do with its unity. One type of unity is ideational (the big idea that the poem asserts). The other part is organizational, and in turn it has two aspects—spatial unity (the underlying contrasts around which the poem is built) and sequential unity (how the poem unfolds from beginning to end).

Putting All the Pieces Together

How to Explicate a Biblical Poem

xplication is the name that literary scholars give to what they call a "close reading" of a poem. It is a standard type of paper that English teachers require of their students. The purpose of this chapter is to impart the information that will enable a person to write the best possible explication of a biblical poem.

Who will benefit from this information? The ones who have the most to gain are high school or college students who wish to master one of the types of papers they are likely to be assigned. But this chapter has something for all readers of biblical poetry. The methodology that I will impart is exactly the right one to use when composing a directed Bible study of a poem, or a sermon that takes a poem as the text. It is also the basis for an inductive Bible study, where the explication needs to be turned into a series of questions to ask of a group. Even in the less formal situation of reading a biblical poem for personal devotions or edification, our experience of a poem will be much richer if we engage in at least some of the analysis that makes up an explication of a poem. Much of this methodology can become second nature to us as we read biblical poems.

What Is an Explication of a Poem?

The dictionary definition of the word "explication" is "explanation," with the implication of *detailed* explanation. The verb form, "explicate," is defined as "to give a detailed explanation and develop the implications," usually in regard to a work of literature (and especially a poem). The etymology of the word points in the direction of the word cluster, "to unfold, make clear, or unravel."

An explication of a poem is a general "reading" of the poem, with the word "reading" implying both description and interpretation. A good explication of a poem does everything with it that will yield an optimal understanding of the poem. An explication is not a thesis paper, though it might form part of a thesis paper. An explication enacts the ideal reading experience of a poem in a general way. The whole poem is in view, not simply a specific aspect of it (as in a thesis paper). We might say that *an explicator does not have a thesis to prove but a poem to unfold.*

Two additional points need to be made. The first is that an explication is a carefully organized close reading, not a bits-and-pieces close reading. It follows a paradigm (to be explained below) that yields the best results. An explicator is a travel guide through the poem, and the itinerary needs to be systematic and complete.

Second, no one can simply sit down and write a polished explication. Explication needs to be preceded by spadework and analysis. After the individual insights have been assembled, they need to be put into the best possible arrangement for an audience (even if that audience is oneself). We might compare this two-stage process to the work of a detective. First a detective needs to assemble the evidence and understand all aspects of a situation. Then the detective puts the assembled data into an organized format to present to a jury.

Content Core and Structure

The format of an explication involves starting at the global level. First we need to provide a superstructure within which the individual details can find a home. Then we explicate the details. We might compare this to standing in front of a painting in an art gallery. The best starting point is to stand back at a distance to bring the overall subject and general features of the painting into focus. The closer we move toward the painting, the more we see of the details. With an explication, too, we need to start with the overall design, and then look at the details. Three stages of distance from the text can be discerned and applied.

The first stage goes by the name of "content core." It consists of the broadest possible things we can say about a poem. This encompasses all or most of the following considerations:

- *Topic and theme.* The topic might be formulated as an abstract concept, but it might also be a literary motif. In most cases, we can identify both a concept and an experience. Psalm 23, for example, is about God's providence in the lives of those who follow him (a concept), but at the surface or literal level the poem follows the list of the activities that a shepherd performs for his sheep during the course of a typical day (a literary motif). The *theme* of the poem is what the poem says *about* the topic or central experience. The theme of Psalm 23 is the sufficiency of the shepherd's provision, and the contentment that comes from resting in that sufficiency.

- *Explicit or implied situation.* Sometimes the context of a poem is a situation that is external to the poem and needs to be inferred from the poem itself. The external situation in the Song of Solomon is the courtship and marriage of Solomon and a young Shulamite woman. Often there is an implied situation *within* a poem. The implied situation in Psalm 73 is the speaker's crisis in faith occasioned by his envy of the prosperous wicked.
- *Genre.* The opening volley of insights that we codify for ourselves or share with an audience is a "catch-all" of whatever we or others would most benefit from knowing right at the outset. It is useful, therefore, to identify the genre(s) to which a poem belongs. Generic labels are immensely helpful—reflective poem, meditative landscape poem, love poem, praise psalm, prophetic oracle of salvation, apocalyptic "golden age" vision, worship psalm, and so forth.

In addition to the content core, the overarching umbrella of a poem includes its structure. As indicated in the preceding chapter of this book, the structure of a poem is multiple. One type is sequential structure, and it, too, is multiple! Here is a grid for understanding the sequential structure of a biblical poem:

- *Three-part form.* Lyric poems (but not such poetic forms as an apocalyptic vision of the future or a prophetic oracle) have an obvious (even ritualistic) opening and closing. It is useful to note these formal elements and the symmetry that results from them. Often something can be said additionally about the middle of a poem—the presence of a catalog, for example, or the presence of a portrait or description.

- *Theme and variation.* This concept was explained in the preceding chapter. Often the opening or lead-in of the poem expresses the unifying theme or motif; occasionally we ourselves need to supply it. Once we have formulated a statement of it, we need to (1) isolate the successive units of the poem and (2) formulate a label for each one in keeping with the announced unifying motif.

- *An outline of the poem.* Every poem has its own, unique-to-it outline as it unfolds from beginning to end. No explication of a poem is complete without providing such an outline. In effect the process of laying out the variations on the central theme or motif provides the outline, but I have given this subject a separate heading in order to make explicit that an explication needs to include an outline of the poem. The basis for separating a unit from the preceding one might be (1) a shift of topic, (2) a shift of imagery, or (3) a shift of feeling. Accordingly, the outline of a poem might trace changing topics or ideas, changing images, or changing feelings.

In addition to possessing a sequential structure, most poems also have a spatial structure—the poem as a whole independent of its linear unfolding. This spatial structure on consists of one or more contrasts that organize the poem.

Poetic Texture

The foregoing section has covered the big, overriding aspects of a poem. Identifying this overall framework is like standing back ten or fifteen feet from a painting in an art gallery to see the total design and the big effects. Exploring the poetic texture (the subject of this unit of the chapter) is like standing close to a painting and seeing the details at close range.

The terms "structure" and "texture" come from the world of architecture and internal design. Structure is equivalent to the beams and wallboard that make up the substance of the walls. Texture is equivalent to the paint or wallpaper that we put on the walls.

What, then, makes up poetic texture? The individual words, images, and figures of speech—the language poets use, we called it in earlier chapters in this book. It is this that embodies the actual meanings of a poem. In unpacking the images and figures of speech we clarify what the poet is saying about his chosen subject matter. In any explication, exploring the poetic texture will take by far the most time and space.

How does one incorporate an analysis of poetic texture into an overall explication? We need to start from the premise that the goal of an explication is to enact the ideal reading experience of a poem. Poems unfold sequentially from beginning to end. The wrong way to conduct an analysis of poetic texture is the topical approach—a paragraph on metaphors in the poem, another on symbolism, another on allusions, and so forth.

The right way to explicate poetic texture is to begin at the beginning of the poem and march through it in sequence. If we are writing an explication as a paper for a class, we need to package the material in paragraphs, each with a topic sentence. This takes analysis and ingenuity, but it pays big dividends. Whether we are arranging our explication by paragraphs or in an informal and fluid manner, we need to isolate units for analysis. At the very least, the units that we identify as variations on the central theme require separate treatment, but often it is useful to isolate smaller units. Even a single image or metaphor might need to be treated as a unit.

The cardinal rule is to progress through the poem in sequence, unit by unit. Additionally, when we come to a given unit, we must *do everything with that unit that it asks to have done with it.* Our goal is to enact the best possible description and interpretation of the poem as it unfolds. We want to explore and delineate all of the important nuances of the text. That can happen only if we fully probe every unit of a poem as we experience it in a sequential reading of the poem. Explication of a poem is a form of literary *commentary* on it, and the standard format for commentary is to be exhaustive with a unit before moving on.

Toward an Explication of Psalm 46

As we now undertake examples of explication, it will be obvious that this chapter is a summary and recapitulation of all the previous chapters in this book. An explication incorporates all of the elements that have been assembled piecemeal in the previous chapters. The new element consists of bringing these elements together in a coherent and organized format. Psalm 46 possesses an ideal brevity and complexity to serve us for a specimen explication.

> [1] God is our refuge and strength,
>> a very present help in trouble.
> [2] Therefore we will not fear though the earth gives way,
>> though the mountains be moved into the
>> heart of the sea,
> [3] though its waters roar and foam,
>> though the mountains tremble at its swelling.
> [4] There is a river whose streams make glad the city of God,
>> the holy habitation of the Most High.
> [5] God is in the midst of her; she shall not be moved;
>> God will help her when morning dawns.
> [6] The nations rage, the kingdoms totter;
>> he utters his voice, the earth melts.
> [7] The LORD of hosts is with us;
>> the God of Jacob is our fortress.

⁸Come, behold the works of the LORD,
> how he has brought desolations on the earth.
⁹He makes wars cease to the end of the earth;
> he breaks the bow and shatters the spear;
> he burns the chariots with fire.
¹⁰"Be still, and know that I am God.
> I will be exalted among the nations,
> I will be exalted in the earth!"
¹¹The LORD of hosts is with us;
> the God of Jacob is our fortress.

The following material is not packaged as a formal written explication but as an illustration of the ingredients of an explication, and it is accordingly presented as a series of bulleted items.

- *Content core*
    - *Genre*: Psalm 46 is an affective lyric poem. It is not a dispassionate meditation on a subject but a highly charged emotional display of feelings and responses to the subject.
    - *Topic:* The certainty of God's presence amid troubling times.
    - *Theme in the ideational sense* (what the poem says *about* the certainty of God's presence amid troubling times): We are freed from fear as we trust in God's presence amid troubling times.
    - *Unifying motif* (*theme in the literary sense*): A catalog of God's protecting actions.
    - *Recognizable human experience*: What it *feels like* to trust God amid troubling times.

- *Underlying contrasts* (spatial structure): God versus forces of disruption or chaos; the stability of God's presence versus instability in all other areas of life; peace of mind versus the things that would induce fear; and the destructiveness in nature and human history versus the redemptiveness of God's salvation history.

- *Sequential structure*
  - o *Three-part structure*: We should note first that the poet anchors his main theme in statements that appear at the beginning of the poem, in the middle of the poem, and at the end of the poem, providing an obvious symmetry. Those units are verses 1, 7, and 11. Usually we find similar material at the beginning and end, but Psalm 46 puts it in the middle as well.
  - o *The three main units* (an outline for the poem), based on changes in imagery: God's presence amid cataclysmic upheaval in nature (vv. 1–3); God's protection in the midst of political and military threats (vv. 4–7); and God's decisive and final defeat of earthly warfare (probably an eschatological vision of the end times). The emphasis of the concluding unit is on the final and universal nature of God's defeat of the warring nations.

- *Poetic texture*: This is what actually embodies the meanings of the poem. Instead of conducting an actual analysis of the poetic texture of Psalm 46, I have decided to list the ingredients that constitute the "terms of engagement" for exploring the poetic texture of poems (most but not all of the following items appear in Psalm 46):
  - o image (also called imagery)
  - o metaphor and simile
  - o allusion
  - o symbol

- o   hyperbole
- o   paradox
- o   apostrophe
- o   connotation
- o   metonymy (substitute naming)
- o   synecdoche (a part that stands for the whole)

- *Verse form (parallelism)*: Parallelism has become some-thing of an orphan after an earlier chapter devoted to it; this is the right place to put it back into circulation. Obviously it serves no useful purpose to say something about parallelism with every verse of a poem. However, whenever parallelism contributes significantly to the meaning, it should be discussed along with other aspects of poetic texture wherever it is in effect part of that texture. For example, there are multiple points in Psalm 46 where the repetitiveness in parallel clauses either has a cumulative effect (e.g., vv. 2–3) or lends an aura of decisiveness or finality to an action (e.g., v. 9). In verse 6, four brief parallel clauses have a hammer-like effect, and additionally two clauses that narrate what the warring nations do are countered by two clauses that narrate what God does. Another dimension of parallelism (especially prominent in Psalm 46) is the artistry and beauty that it adds to a poem. The logical place to celebrate this might be an add-on paragraph after the explication of poetic texture is complete.

LEARNING BY DOING

Psalm 1 possesses the winsome quality of having a surface simplicity that makes it accessible and an actual complexity that elicits our best effort of analysis. The paradigm that produces a good explication has been clearly laid out multiple times in this chapter, so it does not need to be repeated here. Psalm 1 reads as follows:

[1] Blessed is the man
> who walks not in the counsel of the wicked,
nor stands in the way of sinners,
> nor sits in the seat of scoffers;
[2] but his delight is in the law of the LORD,
> and on his law he meditates day and night.
[3] He is like a tree
> planted by streams of water
that yields its fruit in its season,
> and its leaf does not wither.
In all that he does, he prospers.
[4] The wicked are not so,
> but are like chaff that the wind drives away.
[5] Therefore the wicked will not stand in the judgment,
> nor sinners in the congregation of the righteous;
[6] for the LORD knows the way of the righteous,
> but the way of the wicked will perish.

Final Thoughts on Explicating Poetry

Explicating a poem is the opposite of "tearing a poem apart" (the incorrect formula sometimes attached to close reading of a poem). When we explicate a poem we are actually putting the poem together. In fact, we are following the cues provided by the poem and are collaborating with the poet in composing the poem. We are following the same process that the poet followed when composing the poem. To conduct an explication is to undertake a journey of discovery. After making a series of discoveries, we are in a position to be a travel guide to the poem for others who wish to master the poem.

The underlying premise of this chapter is that there is a right way to organize an explication of a poem. By implication, there are also wrong ways to conduct it. We can think of the right paradigm as the "T-formation." The top bar of the T is overview commentary—considerations that apply to the whole poem and that, having been stated, provide a framework into which the close-up view of the poetic texture can be place. This overview material includes the content core of the poem and its structure. Together those things constitute the unity of the poem.

The vertical bar of the T-formation is the sequential reading of the poem, unit by unit. Once we make it clear to ourselves or an audience that we intend to look at the poetic texture in the order in which the poem unfolds, everyone knows exactly what to expect. There are no surprises, and we certainly avoid the confusion that sets it with a disorganized jumping around (as in a "little of this and little of that" approach).

If we are presenting an explication as a directed Bible study, a paper in an English course, or a sermon, the T-formation almost inevitably becomes the I-formation. In those situations, we do not simply end our explication but round it off with a note of finality and closure. In the bottom bar of the I, we move from explication to application, for example, drawing out the implications for daily living. In a written explication for a literature course, it would be appropriate to round off the explication with a recapitulation of main points or a statement of appreciation of what the poet has accomplished or an observation about the universal human experiences embodied in the poem (a hint as to how the poem can become a treasured possession).

Anyone who follows the recommended format for explicating a poem will have met the following rules that govern a good explication:

- provide a big picture before moving to close-ups,
- conduct a close reading of the poem,
- enact the ideal reading experience of the poem as it unfolds from beginning to end,
- produce a unified impression of the poem (partly by being organized itself),
- keep the focus on the text and not escaping to context,
- state analytic insights instead of merely paraphrasing the poem.

Anyone who does those things can be commended for "rightly dividing the word of truth" (2 Tim. 2:15, KJV).

Summary

Producing a good explication of a poem is a grand achievement, and it is within the reach of anyone who simply applies the right methodology. The checklist that concludes the preceding unit describes what a good explication does. The underlying principles of those activities can be summarized this way: a good explication is (1) systematic (it follows a prescribed format), (2) well organized (instead of being a collection of fragments), and (3) comprehensive (it covers all important aspects of a poem).

What Are the Main Types of Psalms?

This book began by looking at *poetry*—the language poets use. The material covered there applied to all poetry in the Bible—narrative poetry in the book of Job, prophetic poetry (including the oracles of judgment and oracles of redemption) in the Old Testament prophetic books, and figures of speech in prose passages all through the Bible. When the subject turned to *poems*, the focus narrowed, as the concept of poem was defined as *lyric poem*. In effect that material applied to the book of Psalms, the Song of Solomon, a few scattered lyrics elsewhere, and the Christ hymns of the New Testament.

In this chapter the focus is even more limited. The assumption of most readers who read the title of this book is that the book will explore how to read and interpret the Psalms. That is not an illegitimate assumption, since the Psalms are what most people most immediately think of when the poetry of the Bible is mentioned. While many other poetic parts of the Bible might have formed chapters in this book, I want to provide my parting help to readers and interpreters of the Psalms.

Several distinct (and distinctive) genres appear in the book of Psalms. As I provide the information about these subtypes, this information should not be regarded as replacing the rules given in preceding chapters. They are instead an extra overlay that we need to place on the material. This extra overlay has to do with the format and content of the poems. All that was said earlier about content core, structure, and texture remains fully operative. Above all, this new information has most of its effect on how the poems are structured. We still need to be looking for three-part structure and theme and variation, but the forms discussed in this chapter are likely to determine how we formulate theme and variation.

I have made the following adjustment to the format for this chapter: after providing an explanation of a given subtype, I will provide an example. I intend this as a "learning by doing" unit and expect my readers to apply what I have said to the specimen that I print.

Lament Psalm

Lament psalms are the most numerous category in the Psalter (the name for the book of 150 psalms). Sometimes the authors of the lament psalms use the generic label *complaint* to identify the type of poem they are composing. Writers of lament psalms wrote in an awareness that the genre consists of five elements, as follows:

- An invocation or cry to God, often accompanied by exalted epithets (titles) for God and sometimes already incorporating an element of petition.
- The lament or complaint, consisting of a definition or description of the crisis surrounding the poem. Usually the poet paints a vivid portrait of evildoers and catalogs their wicked actions.
- Petition or supplication in which the poet asks God to do specific things to correct the crisis.

- A statement of confidence in God.
- A vow to praise God (or sometimes actual praise of God).

We need to note three very important things about the fore-going paradigm: (1) the five elements can appear in any order (even though the order as printed above is the standard one); (2) a given element might appear more than once in a poem; and (3) an element might be omitted from a poem. It is important not to force a lament psalm into a pattern that is not actually present in the text simply because we know that most lament psalms have five parts.

The heart of the lament psalm is the complaint (the descrip-tion of the crisis). This lament section almost always unleashes an abundance of vivid imagery and poetic energy. Lament psalms are occasional poems (poems occasioned by an event in life), and ascer-taining the event can help explain the specific content and tech-nique of a poem. The statement of confidence in God and the vow to praise him produce the effect of a recantation of what the poet has said earlier in the poem: the situation is not hopeless after all. Lament psalms belong to a large branch of literature known as *pro-test literature*. The underlying movement of a lament psalm is the quest, as the poet searches for a solution to an unbearable problem.

Psalm 64 is a brief, "quick hit" example of a lament psalm and provides a good opportunity for you to apply what has just been said about the genre:

> ¹Hear my voice, O God, in my complaint;
>> preserve my life from dread of the enemy.
> ²Hide me from the secret plots of the wicked,
>> from the throng of evildoers,
> ³who whet their tongues like swords,
>> who aim bitter words like arrows,
> ⁴shooting from ambush at the blameless,
>> shooting at him suddenly and without fear.

⁵They hold fast to their evil purpose;
>> they talk of laying snares secretly,
> thinking, "Who can see them?"
⁶   They search out injustice,
> saying, "We have accomplished a diligent search."
>> For the inward mind and heart of a man are
>> deep.
⁷But God shoots his arrow at them;
>> they are wounded suddenly.
⁸They are brought to ruin, with their own tongues
> turned against them;
>> all who see them will wag their heads.
⁹Then all mankind fears;
>> they tell what God has brought about
>> and ponder what he has done.
¹⁰Let the righteous one rejoice in the LORD
>> and take refuge in him!
> Let all the upright in heart exult!

Praise Psalm

The second largest subtype in the Psalter is the psalm of praise. Like the lament psalm, it is a fixed form, meaning that it has specific ingredients that the poet knew needed to be included. The three elements that make up a praise psalm are the following:

- A formal call to praise, which can include as many as three elements: one or more commands to praise God; naming the audience that is commanded to praise; and naming the mode of praise (such as song, lyre, harp).
- The praise itself. Often the transition word "for" stands between the opening call to praise and the catalog of praiseworthy acts and attributes that explain why God should be praised.

- Rounding out praise with a note of closure or resolution. Often this is a concluding prayer or wish.

Obviously this is a specific manifestation of three-part lyric structure that has figured prominently in earlier chapters of this book.

The overall logic of the praise psalm is twofold: to ascribe praise to God and assemble evidence regarding why God is worthy of praise. The word "praise" originally meant to *appraise,* or set a value on something. From this came the meaning of commending the worth of someone or something. Praise is a response to the worthiness of someone or something, and in the psalms of praise this person is God.

The central technique in most praise psalms is the *catalog* of God's praiseworthy acts and attributes. Occasionally this is replaced by a *portrait* of God. As noted in an earlier chapter, a catalog requires us to divide it into its constituent parts, based on changing topics or images. Determining the units in a catalog of praise is likely to constitute a major part of the time we spend on a praise psalm. Some further considerations that operate in a praise psalm include the following:

- The poet can praise God for either his acts or his attributes.
- Sometimes the poet praises God for particular, once-only acts, and at other times for repeated or habitual acts.
- God's praiseworthy acts occur in three primary arenas—nature or creation, history, and the personal life of a believer. Within these arenas, the most common actions for which God is praised are acts of providence, redemption or salvation or forgiveness, creation of the world, and preservation of physical life (either through provision or rescue/deliverance).
- Sometimes the writer of a praise psalm uses generalization, while at other times he cites specific examples (usually the two alternate back and forth in a poem).

- Allusion (reference to past history) looms large as a technique because the impulse is to praise God for acts that he has performed.
- Sometimes the poet praises God for personal blessings, and at other times the focus is public or communal.

LEARNING BY DOING

Psalm 33 is a prototypical praise psalm and provides a good opportunity to learn by doing:

> [1] Shout for joy in the LORD, O you righteous!
>> Praise befits the upright.
> [2] Give thanks to the LORD with the lyre;
>> make melody to him with the harp of ten strings!
> [3] Sing to him a new song;
>> play skillfully on the strings, with loud shouts.
> [4] For the word of the LORD is upright,
>> and all his work is done in faithfulness.
> [5] He loves righteousness and justice;
>> the earth is full of the steadfast love of the LORD.
> [6] By the word of the LORD the heavens were made,
>> and by the breath of his mouth all their host.
> [7] He gathers the waters of the sea as a heap;
>> he puts the deeps in storehouses.
> [8] Let all the earth fear the LORD;
>> let all the inhabitants of the world stand in
>> awe of him!
> [9] For he spoke, and it came to be;
>> he commanded, and it stood firm.
> [10] The LORD brings the counsel of the nations to nothing;
>> he frustrates the plans of the peoples.

[11] The counsel of the LORD stands forever,
        the plans of his heart to all generations.
[12] Blessed is the nation whose God is the LORD,
        the people whom he has chosen as his heritage!
[13] The LORD looks down from heaven;
        he sees all the children of man;
[14] from where he sits enthroned he looks out
        on all the inhabitants of the earth,
[15] he who fashions the hearts of them all
        and observes all their deeds.
[16] The king is not saved by his great army;
        a warrior is not delivered by his great strength.
[17] The war horse is a false hope for salvation,
        and by its great might it cannot rescue.
[18] Behold, the eye of the LORD is on those who fear him,
        on those who hope in his steadfast love,
[19] that he may deliver their soul from death
        and keep them alive in famine.
[20] Our soul waits for the LORD;
        he is our help and our shield.
[21] For our heart is glad in him,
        because we trust in his holy name.
[22] Let your steadfast love, O LORD, be upon us,
        even as we hope in you.

Worship Psalm

A worship psalm is also known as a song of Zion. The distinguishing feature of a worship psalm is its content: it takes worshiping God in the temple as its subject matter. The situation is as simple as that. The overall logic of a worship psalm is twofold: the poem awakens a longing to worship God and expresses the joy of engaging in that worship.

Like lament psalms, worship psalms are *occasional poems*, meaning that they arise from a specific event in the poet's life. The occasion of the songs of Zion was going on pilgrimages to Jerusalem and worshiping God at the temple. Because of this, the physical sense of place is prominent in worship psalms. Praise of the city of Jerusalem is a common motif, as the city itself unleashes the wellsprings of emotion. It is customary for the poet to rehearse the physical details of the temple experience.

As a result, the worship psalms are replete with "snapshots" of what it was like to worship God in the temple. Accompanying these snapshots are pervasive exclamations that allow us to vicariously experience the feelings that pulsed through the Old Testament worshiper. Since pilgrimages to Jerusalem were a required part of the worship experience, the pilgrimage motif is also a common ingredient in the songs of Zion; in fact, Psalms 120–134 are "songs of ascent," that is, pilgrim psalms that were sung or chanted or reflected on during the journey "up" to Jerusalem to worship in the temple. Psalm 84 is the prototypical worship psalm:

> [1] How lovely is your dwelling place,
>> O LORD of hosts!
> [2] My soul longs, yes, faints
>> for the courts of the LORD;
> my heart and flesh sing for joy
>> to the living God.
> [3] Even the sparrow finds a home,
>> and the swallow a nest for herself,
>> where she may lay her young,
> at your altars, O LORD of hosts,
>> my King and my God.
> [4] Blessed are those who dwell in your house,
>> ever singing your praise!

⁵Blessed are those whose strength is in you,
        in whose heart are the highways to Zion.
⁶As they go through the Valley of Baca
        they make it a place of springs;
        the early rain also covers it with pools.
⁷They go from strength to strength;
        each one appears before God in Zion.
⁸O LORD God of hosts, hear my prayer;
        give ear, O God of Jacob!
⁹Behold our shield, O God;
        look on the face of your anointed!
¹⁰For a day in your courts is better
        than a thousand elsewhere.
I would rather be a doorkeeper in the house of my God
        than dwell in the tents of wickedness.
¹¹For the LORD God is a sun and shield;
        the LORD bestows favor and honor.
No good thing does he withhold
        from those who walk uprightly.
¹²O LORD of hosts,
        blessed is the one who trusts in you!

Nature Poems and Nature Poetry

There are five nature poems in the Psalter, but nature finds its way into dozens of additional psalms. As a result, we need to think of nature *poetry* as well as nature *poems*. A nature poem is identifiable by its subject matter, namely, some aspect of external nature.

Nature poetry typically shares the following traits: the poet praises nature for its beauty, power, and provision; the poet describes nature in evocative word pictures that awaken our own experiences of nature; and the poet personifies aspects of nature to show kinship between people and nature. The overall logic that governs a nature psalm is the twofold purpose of expressing and awakening our sense of the glory of (1) nature and (2) the God of nature. The nature poetry of the world at large does the first of those only, whereas the nature psalms continuously deflect the praise upward from nature to God.

Additionally, much of what we find in the nature psalms will fall into place if we are aware of the twofold context out of which the poets wrote: (1) they belonged to a nation of farmers in which nearly everyone lived close to the soil and the weather, and (2) they had a thoroughgoing doctrine of creation that asserted that God had created everything that exists. The following excerpt from Psalm 147 will enable you to see how the foregoing generalizations find their way into the nature poetry of the Psalter:

> [7]Sing to the LORD with thanksgiving;
>> make melody to our God on the lyre!
> [8]He covers the heavens with clouds;
>> he prepares rain for the earth;
>> he makes grass grow on the hills.
> [9]He gives to the beasts their food,
>> and to the young ravens that cry.
> [10]His delight is not in the strength of the horse,
>> nor his pleasure in the legs of a man,
> [11]but the LORD takes pleasure in those who fear him,
>> in those who hope in his steadfast love.
> [12]Praise the LORD, O Jerusalem!
>> Praise your God, O Zion!
> [13]For he strengthens the bars of your gates;
>> he blesses your children within you.
> [14]He makes peace in your borders;
>> he fills you with the finest of the wheat.
> [15]He sends out his command to the earth;
>> his word runs swiftly.

^{16}He gives snow like wool;

he scatters frost like ashes.

^{17}He hurls down his crystals of ice like crumbs;

who can stand before his cold?

^{18}He sends out his word, and melts them;

he makes his wind blow and the waters flow.

The foregoing excerpt comes from a nature psalm. The nature poetry of the passage is intermingled with other material, but even this is part of the total meaning of the passage considered as nature poetry.

Final Thoughts on Types of Psalms

Several things need to be said at this point to avoid possible misconceptions. The four psalm types discussed in this chapter are the most frequently occurring ones, but they do not make up the entire Psalter by any means. Together they make up perhaps sixty or seventy percent of the Psalter. This means that many psalms are just plain lyric poems. Furthermore, one can do a creditable job with the four types discussed in this chapter by treating them as generic poems. However, not to apply the more specific grid of a given subtype would be to cut against the grain and not quite do justice to the specificity of the text.

Further qualifications also need to be stated. Some psalms lack a formal call to praise but in other ways follow the rules of a praise psalm by listing God's praiseworthy acts and attributes, and by ascribing praise to God. It would not be at all wrong to treat these psalms under the rubric of praise psalms.

Additionally and very importantly, a given psalm might *show affinities to* a given subtype without actually belonging to that genre. Thus it is entirely possible that in a given section of a poem we will find passages that correspond to elements of a lament psalm or a nature poem. It is appropriate to point this out as part of our explication of those poems, but in these instances it is very important not to label the whole poem as falling into a subtype.

For example, I have marveled at how many of my students label Psalm 73 a lament psalm. It is not such, but it has parts that resemble a lament psalm. It paints an extended portrait of the prosperous wicked, and that portrait would be right at home in a lament psalm (inasmuch as the portrait of the wicked is prominent in lament psalms). However, in Psalm 73 the poet does not complain about the prosperous wicked but envies them. Again, Psalm 73 ends with the line "that I may tell of all your works." That perhaps ranks as a vow to praise God, but it does not make Psalm 73 a lament psalm. The interpretive rule is never to force a psalm into a genre to which it does not fully fit. If a poem does not fully fit a generic category, the right procedure is to treat it as a generic "poem" (meaning lyric poem), and then name affinities to a more specific subtype in regard to specific passages in the poem.

A final explanation is this: a nature poem or lament psalm or whatever is a poem first of all, and after that it is a specific subtype. The forms covered in this chapter give us an additional overlay of considerations. Regardless of what subtype a poem represents, interpreting the poetic texture remains the thing that embodies the meanings of the poem, and analyzing it takes the same form for all poems.

Summary

The optimal experience of a poem requires that before we finish with the poem we look at it in terms of its most specific generic traits, and not only in terms of more general traits. Not that we should ignore the general traits; they need to be part of our analysis. But we need to bring the considerations of lament psalm, praise psalm, worship psalm, and nature poetry to bear on poems that fall into these categories.